$100,000 and Above

and Above

*The New Realities of
the Executive Job Market*

By Bob Gerberg
Princeton/Masters Press

Personal thanks are extended to Lew Turner, Tom Smith, Bob West, Michele Lutz, and Bob Schrier. Their experiences and successes in marketing six figure executives were of great value in helping assemble this book.

Library of Congress Catalog Card Number 95-92429

ISBN 1-822885-04-X (cloth)

Attention Businesses:
Books by Princeton/Masters Press are available at quantity discounts.
For information, write: Princeton/Masters Press Inc., 7951 E.
Maplewood, Suite 333, Englewood, CO 80111 or call 800-772-4446.

5 4 3 2 1

About the Author

Bob Gerberg has a BA degree from Colgate University and an MBA degree from the University of Pittsburgh. After several years as an Air Force officer, he had a successful career with major food companies, including positions as a Vice President of Marketing and Assistant to the Chairman of a Fortune 500 company.

Active in the career and outplacement fields for more than a decade, he has authored more than two dozen books, publications and cassettes on the subjects of job and career change. He is also the creator of the Princeton/Masters International concept for marketing six-figure executives.

About Princeton Masters

Princeton/Masters is an outplacement consulting firm with offices and associates in major cities. The firm's specialty is in helping market high-level professionals and executives into new jobs and careers.

When people talk to me about their executive careers, invariably I am often amazed by how many people feel they are just getting by on their six-figure incomes. Large mortgages, concerns about aging parents, higher college tuitions, and more expensive leisure pursuits have more people than ever thinking about new jobs or careers.

When it comes to career search they want to know…How long will it take me to find the right position? Or, how will I do with recruiters? Or, should I mail my resume as widely as possible? While common-sense answers are an unqualified yes, the correct answers are rather different in today's reality, and they are among the points addressed in this book.

The typical executive doesn't seek employment very often… and is, quite frankly, not much good at it. Unfortunately, the reality of the marketplace is that there are hundreds of applicants for every choice situation. So, you can let this depress you. Or you can do something about it.

As a six-figure executive, you stand to lose $2,000, $3,000, $4,000 or more every week that you may be out of work. You also stand to lose a substantial amount, every week, if you are unhappy with your career, or are working for compensation that is below what you are really worth.

This book is based upon our experiences at Princeton / Masters International in working with thousands of men and women in search of six-figure executive positions. It's about what we've observed that works… and what doesn't. I wish to thank the several hundred recruiters, HR Directors, Princeton / Masters clients and staff who have shared their observations, and many are quoted in this book. Others requested anonymity as the comments they offered were personal and were not provided on behalf of their employers. With my best wishes for your success,

Bob Gerberg

Table of Contents

— 1 —

What Is Today's Job Market at $100,000 and Above?

Is it good and growing? Or, is it more competitive than ever?

The new reality: The numbers have changed dramatically. Yes, more executive jobs... but the number of competitors has accelerated at a faster pace. If you haven't looked for a job in a while, it's a whole new ball game.

*I*t's no surprise that millions of executives are finding themselves in jobs or careers that they no longer enjoy, and that bring them far less than they really want out of life.

Our jobs affect our feelings, our moods, our families, our energy and even our whole outlook on life. They also change the way we see ourselves and the way others see us.

Unfortunately, when it comes to careers, many executives across the globe play it safe. They tend to underestimate themselves and therefore put up with jobs that offer little future or excitement. These people have stopped growing. Furthermore, they won't grow, simply because they won't give themselves a chance.

Why? Well, it's easier to stay with what is familiar than risk the unknown. It's also hard to overcome inertia and take that first step.

"I see a great many quotes from executives and the media that are off-base. They talk about a perceived scarcity of six-figure jobs, but it's just not the case.

The number of executive jobs and the amounts of executive pay are both expanding at a very nice rate. The problem for people looking is that the number of job seekers out there is growing a lot faster."
—*Larry Mingle, Executive Recruiter, Formerly with Norman Broadbent and Russell Reynolds Associates*

However, one of the great lessons about jobs and careers is that by virtue of education and experience, we each have a reservoir of talents and skills that are unknown or untapped. What's more, this unused potential has been proven to exist at virtually all ages.

How many $100,000 jobs are there?

The job market at this level has changed dramatically in recent years. While it has grown, it has become far more competitive than ever before.

With a U.S. population of more than 260,000,000 people, and a total job market approaching 130,000,000, opportunities for those seeking to earn more than $100,000 are very limited.

Here are the number of jobs in the U.S. that currently reward people with salaries, commissions and bonuses at this level (the income figures are exclusive of revenues received from interest, dividends and capital gains):

2,512,000 jobs at $100K — $199K ..   (1.90%)
636,000 jobs at $200K — $499K ..   (0.50%)
122,000 jobs at $500K — $999K ..   (0.10%)
58,000 jobs at $1,000K + ... (0.04%)

Interestingly enough, the number of jobs at this level is increasing at a fairly rapid rate. Over the last five years, while much of the U.S. was in a fairly severe recession, the six-figure job market grew more than 27%.

Obviously, modest inflation contributes to this; nevertheless, based on these statistics, the market for six-figure executives might sound very attractive.

I should also note that a significant percentage of the people earning this level of income are doctors, lawyers, consultants, entertainment industry types (including authors and those associated with professional athletics) and entrepreneurs who run their own companies.

However, there exists an equal number of people who have real earnings at this level but fail to report much of their income, as they take advantage of substantial perks and expenses rather than receiving pure wages.

Now, because many of the six-figure positions are increasingly held by entrepreneurs, of these three million plus jobs, the best estimate is that 27,000 (0.8%) are now coming available each month—a declining percentage of employment at this level.

In recent years, there has been less turnover and executives are working to more advanced ages. Additionally, a small number of jobs become available through newly created positions.

Where are the six-figure jobs...
in small or large organizations?

If your goal is to make the best possible career move rather than simply getting a job, and if you want to do it faster than others, it's important to have some perspective on just where the opportunities are in today's market.

During the last decade there has been a profound change in America. The most, and often the best, opportunities are with smaller businesses rather than with blue chip companies.

"In 1995, 3,000,000 new U.S. jobs will be created. However, firms with over 5,000 employees will account for only 6%; and those with more than 100 employees will only account for 34% of these. Small business continues to be where the growth is."
—Dun & Bradstreet Survey

Among large firms, because annual turnover is estimated to be 25%, many positions are always becoming available. Nevertheless, if we discount mergers, total six-figure employment in the country's 2,000 largest employers has not increased over the last ten years.

Obviously, there will continue to be many fine opportunities that become available with the nation's leading organizations; however, in many cases they will only occur from retirements, terminations, and turnover.

On the other hand, despite the bad news that is so often the focus of the business press, the fact remains that the U.S. has hundreds of expanding industries.

Because well over 90% of all executives who look for jobs want to reside in their current geographic areas, the following statistics will give you some idea of the number of employers out there for you—aside from the national headquarters of better known and larger organizations.

Let's look at two major metropolitan areas. Here's the number of employers in San Francisco/Oakland, which have a combined population of 3.8 million:

111,000 have under 5 employees;
50,000 have 5 to 99 employees;
2,200 have more than 100.

The number of employers in Houston, with a population of 3.4 million, is as follows:

83,000 have under 5 employees;
48,000 have 5 to 99 employees;
2,100 have more than 100.

Obviously, the organizations that have fewer than five employees will be of little interest. However, the employers with between five and 100 employees includes companies in many of America's newest and fastest growing industries. If your career has been rooted in large companies, then some new thinking might be in order.

How much competition
is there for six-figure jobs?

At any one moment in time, the number of executives (and about-to-be executives) who are circulating resumes at this level has grown to exceed *dozens of times* the available positions.

This may be an exaggerated result of continuing uncertainty and concern about executive job security. However, the net result is that today's executive job market is intensely competitive and getting more so.

As organizations become more lean, hundreds of thousands of high-caliber executives compete for what is, on a relative basis, a declining pool of attractive positions. And, as more and more companies are re-engineered, the emphasis on financial pragmatism can only be expected to continue.

"We have no difficulty whatsoever in finding talent for six-figure positions. If you are an expert on derivatives, or a software engineer, you're in high demand. If you're an average lawyer, financial executive, or most anyone else, you've got a major challenge."

—William Oldham,
VP, Investment Banking Company

If you are seeking a new career at this level, you need to understand what you are up against...and what is really needed to find the right job. That's what this book is all about.

By the way, the extent of competition is easily documented as many leading recruiters report the receipt of thousands of unsolicited resumes each month.

When you add the fact that less than 1% of all jobs above $100,000 are advertised, these positions are extremely hard to find. That's why searching with hit-or-miss approaches will invariably lead to disappointment.

Summing Up

The six-figure job market is growing at an average of 6% a year. However, from 1985 to 1995 more than a third of all U.S. companies were restructured; several hundred thousand firms were downsized, and over 100,000 were acquired.

What's more, half a million businesses failed in addition to almost a million that sought bankruptcy protection. The bottom line... there is far more competition for executive jobs than ever before.

You can decide to seek a raise, a promotion or a better type of job where you are, but if you decide to enter the marketplace, you need to draw some completely new boundaries concerning the steps you'll take to get your credentials in front of the right people.

— 2 —

How Do Most Executives Look for Six-Figure Positions?

Are you used to approaches from the 70s and 80s? The ones where you put together a "tombstone" resume, answered some ads, and visited a few recruiters and friends?

The new reality: Out-of-date approaches don't work well in any field and they won't serve you well in a job campaign. Haphazard efforts will have you chasing dead-end leads and job hunting for a long, long time. On the other hand, if you're willing to put your old concepts aside, it's relatively easy to keep control of your own career destiny.

Why do most executives decide to make a move today? Our surveys reveal that 77% of them say that during the last year they had considered looking for a new job; however, most never entered the job market.

Aside from losing a job, the most frequently mentioned reasons for thinking about a move include the following: not getting along with my boss; passed over; not in mainstream; enjoy my job but wish to try something else; blocked, need higher income; or, my position was changed. Other factors that are commonly mentioned:

boredom; being unchallenged; not having enough enjoy-
ment; being in the wrong field or industry; the company
is contracting; I feel burned out; the political environment
is bad; and, the pressure is too high.

Do you know how most executives look for jobs... and how they find them?

Unfortunately, the brutal truth is this: There are several
dozens and even hundreds of applicants for every "average job" at this level.

> *"Most executives are totally unprepared
> to market themselves. Many do virtually
> nothing. They rely on a few select contacts
> to help and lose thousands of dollars in
> the process."*
>
> *—Bill Kaiser, Divisional VP HR,*
> *Detergent Manufacturer*

People start by preparing a "tombstone resume" that
typically says, "Here lies John Doe, went to these schools,
had these executive jobs." Then, once they get their resumes together, they just scatter them as they answer
some ads or visit a few recruiters or personal contacts.

Some send out mass mailings using poor materials,
the wrong lists, and the wrong techniques. In short, their
approach is haphazard, full of dead-end leads, and they
end up job hunting for a long, long time.

Even when they land a new position, the vast majority
look upon the career search as a difficult process in which
they found their way by trial and error. Among those who
make changes, the way in which their "traditional methods" enable them to find their positions may surprise you:

.... *60% from existing contacts and direct referrals;*
.... *22% from networking efforts (indirect referrals);*
.... *9% through contact with executive recruiters;*
.... *5% from contacting employers directly;*
.... *3% by all other means;*
.... *1% through answering advertisements.*

How long does it take
to find jobs at $100,000 and above?

The statistics below summarize the recent average experience, without professional help, of men and women in search of six-figure positions. Incidentally, the majority of these people ended up accepting lesser positions.

Among the executives surveyed who had been forced out of work via downsizing and who did not have outplacement help, here is the average number of months from the date of their notification until they started in a new job:

Scientific	*20.7*
General Management	*17.7*
Legal / Consulting	*16.6*
Human Resources	*15.9*
Accounting / Finance	*15.1*
Misc. Staff Positions	*14.9*
Operations	*14.7*
Office Management	*13.8*
Marketing / Sales / PR	*13.8*
Engineering & Related	*12.3*
Information Systems.	*12.1*

This was during a slow economy; however, the main reason it took them so long was primarily due to their lack of a professional marketing approach and their dependence on their own contacts. Many of them were also in situations that dictated a change in careers or a move into a new industry, but they were reluctant to try and make a move. Even though many had thought about making a move for 12 to 18 months, it was still surprising how many were caught short when finally faced with termination.

Surprisingly, even though their unemployment would eventually cost them an average of between $8,000 and $24,000+ per month, relatively few privately invested any real money toward finding their new jobs!

"On the average, I think the hidden reality is that it takes six-figure executives 1.5 months for every $10,000 they are seeking, but no one is going to admit it."

—*Lance Wright, HR,*
Mobile Oil

Clearly, executive job hunting does not need to take as long as the data on the previous page suggests. However, in a recent major article, *Business Week* magazine said executives who lost jobs should plan on 18 months of unemployment, and the U.S. Labor Department has been widely quoted as saying it takes a year.

Does executive job hunting
require any new steps today?

Up until now, most executives have allowed their lives to be determined by jobs that simply come their way at a point in time. Typically, they may have engaged in "passive" job hunting, where they wait for ads to appear or for recruiters or contacts to call.

Now, of course, major employers will continue to downsize and to thin management ranks for years. In this environment of faded corporate loyalty and much greater competition, how should you approach your next career move?

The starting point is to recognize that the revolution in personal computers, word processing, databases, and other sources for information can have a dramatic and positive impact on your potential for job-hunting success.

These things are part of what makes it possible for you to take control of your own destiny instead of playing the waiting game. It's with this in mind that our philosophy is designed to give you a more strategic approach toward maximizing every job-hunting action you take.

I believe in an approach that clearly emphasizes new and well-organized approaches for going to your markets. The goal is to uncover the right opportunities within a less competitive environment. I call it "pro-active" rather than passive job hunting.

At Princeton/Masters we've learned that for executives and professionals, job hunting has become a highly specialized skill, and we believe in a planned approach to everything you do as part of your job campaign.

There are four broad stages. The first thing you need to do is to make sure you uncover all your marketable assets, and that you clearly know what your career and industry options are. Too many people write a resume before they have ever really analyzed themselves and the full range of what they might be able to offer an employer in certain situations.

In line with this, you need to make sure you uncover every marketable asset or experience you have. At the same time, you will want to review your career and industry options. When you do this, keep in mind that too often, people view themselves solely by what they've done before, thereby restricting their options before they ever get going.

Many executives have found that crucial career changes have changed their lives and brought them success, and, in some cases, fame. Chances are, you can discover entirely new careers and industries, as well as advanced opportunities within your career path.

"I'm seeing a change in the market. It's getting difficult to find the right six-figure talent from a technical side. From the managerial, finance, or marketing side, there's an unbelievable surplus."
—Carl Bruce, Chief Information Officer, Unisource Corporation

---

The second thing that's required is that you must develop superior creative materials. This is extremely critical. A superior biography can easily have 700% to 1,000% more impact than a standard resume might have achieved.

In this book, you will be introduced to a simple philosophy for preparing superior creative materials... resumes and letters that will produce the level of response you need.

Of course, once you've got your materials, you will need to know what to do with them. Out of our work with thousands of job campaigns, we have evolved a considerable body of knowledge about certain strategies, and what steps need to be taken to get the right interviews. So our third requirement involves having an action plan and knowing how to generate high-level interviews.

The fourth requirement involves interviewing and negotiating. Let's face it, for every situation, there are likely to be a number of executives under consideration. So obviously you must come across better than others.

The most critical thing you need to do here is to build personal chemistry with all the new people you will be meeting. In this book, you'll find a series of steps which, if you follow, will allow you to maximize your chemistry in every interviewing situation.

You'll also be introduced to what I call your "personal communications plan"... a key element in any executive job search. Naturally, negotiating is very important, and you should never be intimidated by the process.

Unfortunately, when some executives receive an offer, they simply take it. The fact is that every year people leave millions of dollars on the bargaining tables.

With that in mind, this book will also introduce you to an easy-to-use process for negotiating your best possible financial package. It has been all that many other executives have needed. I hope it will do the same thing for you.

Using this approach, how do people find jobs?

Typically, people using our system develop interviews from a range of sources. The statistics that follow reflect the source that yielded the final job offer they accepted. Keep in mind that people pursue many methods simultaneously for getting interviews, and they use them in conjunction with superior materials.

The main thing about their efforts is that they become far less dependent on their own personal contacts, as more than 85% find jobs via other avenues. Here is the breakdown:

   ... 39% from contacting employers directly;
   ... 30% from networking efforts (indirect referrals);
   ... 13% from existing contacts and direct referrals;

... 12% through contact with executive recruiters;
..... 2% through answering advertisements;
..... 4% by all other means.

You might compare these numbers with what I gave you on page 17... how executives find their jobs using traditional approaches. Incidentally, we've found that using our approach, most executives can cut their job-hunting time in half, and sometimes by much more.

What is
required for success?

You need to be willing to put aside your old ideas on job hunting, and you need to make a commitment to put the information into action. This is about a process. Once mastered, it will build your self-esteem and confidence.

The most important elements for your success will be your own attitude, your will to succeed and your commitment to spending the time to do it the right way. When most people look for a job, they work on it four to five hours a week. Then, if you add the fact that they go out with the wrong materials and do all the wrong things, what can they realistically expect?

In spite of the competition, don't be misguided by the statistics on how long a six-figure search might take. Experience has shown that you can move quickly and get far better results at the same time.

Summing Up

Job-hunting methods from the 80s don't work very well anymore. But, then again, old marketing approaches don't work in any field. In recent articles, Harvard Business Review on "Marketing is Everything" and Business Week on "Value Marketing" both emphasized that smart marketing requires doing different things. Sony's founder, Masaru Ibuka, said, "The key to success for Sony, and to everything else in business, is never to follow the others." This is also sound advice for every executive job seeker.

— 3 —

Will You Need to Explore New Industry Options?

Are you assured of continued career success in your current industry, or should you be thinking about some insurance?

The new reality: More executives than ever change industries, and many go on to greater success. Don't shortchange yourself by taking a narrow view of your options.

When you're thinking about changing jobs, you need to take a close look at yourself, your career field and the industry you're working in. For better or worse, in our world of work you will quickly find that when compared to a decade ago, you have changed, your career has changed, and your industry has changed.

In today's executive job market the great majority of executives must be prepared to market themselves with sufficient skill so that they may be viewed as attractive to employers in their industries.

Now, if you decide to change industries, your success may have a lot to do with being in a growth area. What are some of the fast-growing industries as we enter the latter half of the 90s? Well, they include such industries as personal computers, software, microchips, entertainment, telecommunications, certain media, biotechnology, physical therapy/fitness, special education, security/private investigation, and sports, to name a few.

In 1982, the personal computer industry was a $1 billion industry. Today, it is estimated to be more than a $150 billion industry. During this period, the industry has had many ups and downs, but total six-figure employment has dramatically expanded.

While many firms have been through profit squeezes and layoffs, an individual who joined this industry during the last decade would now have a substantial range of employer possibilities competing for his or her talents.

"The three hardest industry changes to make are when you're moving out of government... out of education... or out of the armed services. Other industry changes are never easy, but are no longer unusual."

—Patricia Maynard,
HR Consultant, Marriot Hotels

Another major reason for seeking out growth industries involves their need to go outside their industry to meet their employment needs. For example, in the early 80s the cable television industry was beginning a phase of explosive growth. The CEOs of these firms could not find enough executives with cable television experience to to meet their companies' growth objectives.

As a result, opportunities abounded for high-level professionals from many varied backgrounds. These firms simply hired the best natural talent, regardless of their previous areas of expertise.

Eight out of every ten executives who are changing jobs are considering new options in terms of industry. Despite the recession of the early 90s, new companies are springing up throughout America. Established organizations are re-examining the way they do business. Medium-sized companies are expanding. New industries now exist that are employing tens of thousands.

Needless to say, the more you appear to know about an industry, the easier it is to generate interviews. For example, do you have experience in or knowledge of similar product lines, distribution channels, manufacturing methods, or problems within their industry?

There can be other similarities. Consider the scope of operations, the role of advertising and promotion, the importance of the field-sales organization, or the influence of labor.

Naturally, the harder it is to demonstrate knowledge of an industry, the less likely an executive is to make a move into it. This rule applies to all major disciplines: sales, marketing, finance, manufacturing, and operations. It is less important in staff disciplines.

What are the types of industry changes that are commonplace?

A client of ours was a marketing executive with a tobacco company, and she joined a cosmetics firm. Why? Their methods of marketing are similar.

Another client was the executive vice president of a circuit-board company, and was recruited to become president of a firm that makes power packs. Why? These industries have similarities in manufacturing and sales, even though the products are very different.

A well-known executive of an aerospace company was recruited to become CEO of a small firm that sells high-tech services to defense contractors. Why? The key was the new CEO's contacts and his knowledge of the market.

If you have no knowledge of an industry but would like to explore situations, extra steps are recommended. The easiest way to acquire knowledge of a new industry is to read trade publications. They will bring you up to date on personnel changes, new products, information on specific companies and the major challenges as seen by industry leaders.

> *"There isn't a growth industry in America that doesn't hire people from other industries. There's no other solution to our executive staffing requirements."*
>
> *—Robert Nelson,*
> *Senior VP HR, Software Firm*

Another way is to talk with executives already in the field. In some cases, you can go further by getting more formal input, attending trade shows, and the like. The most radical approach is to accept a lower-level job in an industry in order to acquire knowledge.

Why overlook troubled industries?

During the last decade we've witnessed declines in a succession of industries. However, I believe you should never overlook opportunities in troubled industries. Executives who have worked for firms under pressure often find that they can be valuable to distributors or to consulting firms. Those who learned tough lessons in competitive battles can function as veterans in any industry.

As you begin to consider industry options, you'll also need to decide whether you should take a narrow view. This is essential if there are many growth companies in the industries you're searching.

However, if you are part of an industry that is suffering, you will want to adopt a broad view of your options. The more you understand the dynamics of a market, the more you can spot potential opportunities.

Transition is obviously more difficult but still quite possible. Historically, executives tend to overrate the barriers and to underrate their own abilities to make contributions in new areas in a relatively short time frame.

As you review potential industries, remember that while glamorous high-tech and service businesses receive 90% of the publicity today, many executives will find far more opportunities in industries that are considered low-tech or non-glamorous by today's standards.

Can you capitalize on your leverage power, versatility and your ability to contribute?

As you consider new industries, be sure not to overlook your leverage power. Here I am referring to the added benefits you may bring by virtue of your contacts or knowledge. You may be able to bring a complete team with you that helped you "turn around" a similar situation. Perhaps you control major accounts who would switch their business. Or it's possible you have cut millions from overhead before and know exactly how you would do it again.

Your versatility can also be a major consideration. The fact is, nearly every capable executive can work in a different function that is either broader, narrower, or in some way associated with a past position. Here are some examples that will reinforce this point.

A versatile purchasing executive found it easy to move to a position where he is responsible for all manufacturing; and a general manager who came up through marketing in a consumer products division became the marketing VP for another consumer goods company.

A senior executive switched to big-ticket computer sales because of his past experience as a user; and a lending officer in a bank became the top executive in a financial services firm.

"Most executives never identify all the ways they can be of value to employers. But, the key today is being multifaceted. The trick is to stop thinking only of those things for which you had direct responsibility."

—Narisimha Dela,
Management Consultant,
Former VP, Chase Manhattan Intern'l

Be sure to communicate the scope of your knowledge and potential. Sales executives, for instance, usually know quite a bit about marketing, human resources and distribution. Manufacturing executives often know a great deal about administration, finance and general management. A controller may often have a grasp of every aspect of his/her business.

When you are discussing the requirements for a position, it will be important for you to distinguish between arbitrary requirements and those that really relate directly to results. Arbitrary requirements include degrees, length of time in positions, previous titles and specific industry experience.

However, the final hiring decision usually has little to do with specifications. If you can present yourself convincingly as being able to produce results, you will likely get the job. Here are some examples:

An executive went from government to becoming the chairman of a pharmaceutical company; and a lawyer from the steel business became president of an engineering company.

The CEO of a public corporation became president of a large Wall Street firm; and the EVP of a giant utility became chairman of a diversified manufacturer.

There are thousands of examples, and at all income levels. If you believe you can produce direct results in a given situation, be sure you lay claim to it.

Too many executives seek out positions at a lower level than they should, or they rule themselves out of a job they could do well, simply because they have never done it before. Confidence is a critical asset for executives. Don't underrate yourself.

If you are switching industries, you will find that, generally speaking, more opportunities emerge in the small and mid-sized companies. They don't have layers of management waiting to fill new opportunities. Also, their executives tend to be less specialized, making it possible for you to fill a more versatile role.

Summing Up

Many people are afraid to move out of their industry specialty. However, every month thousands of executives start careers in new industries—areas where they had no direct previous experience. Once you've had executive experience in two or three industries, your marketability will be greater than ever before.

— 4 —

Does Your Career Need
to Take a Whole New Direction?

Have you ever thought about making a dramatic career change?

The new reality: Most executives have changed careers more than once. In the future, it will be even more frequent. Interestingly, six-figure executives who make a total career change often select one of seven general options.

As mentioned in the last chapter, executives not only undergo change themselves, but their career fields can change dramatically in the course of a decade. Fields that once offered great opportunity can soon be viewed as financially confining with limited growth possibilities.

Does advertising offer the same career possibilities as it did a decade ago? Does selling in the steel industry? Does being a doctor in the field of sports medicine? Obviously, the answer is no. Career fields not only change, but change occurs at a much faster pace than most executives realize.

Experience has proven that if you take a narrow view of yourself, you could be making a major mistake. If you see yourself as a specialist, you may believe you are locked in to a given career. Or you may feel you have few available options because you are too much of a generalist.

Believe it or not, there are 22,000 different job titles in use today, but 95% of all professionals fall within one of several hundred career specialties.

"Have any of your executives left senior positions and started new careers? I've known five people who have recently done this. Three went into consulting based on their expertise; two started their own businesses. Most executive career changes fit a similar pattern."

—*Greg Larson, Senior HR Manager, Marathon Oil*

By career specialties, I am referring to such areas as: professional fund raiser, executive recruiter, geologist, attorney, politician, stockbroker, and so on. Nevertheless, when six-figure executives make a major career change, they generally choose one of the seven popular options that follow.

(1) Are you interested in a franchise or license agreement?

This has become the standard alternative for hundreds of thousands of executives. The number of franchises available has multiplied dramatically as more than 4,000 companies in 120 industries offer franchises today.

About 1,000,000 investors now account for 30% of our GNP and 40% of all retail sales. The amount of money required to get started in different businesses varies greatly. In most cases, financial help is available.

(2) Do you want to be a
consultant or join a consulting firm?

The field has been expanding at a rapid rate during the past decade. Part of the reason is that the knowledge business as a whole has been booming. If you decide to become a practicing consultant, your perceived professionalism will be very important.

As you probably realize, thousands of executives begin thriving consulting practices each year. However, it rarely happens automatically. The first thing to recognize is that you will need some form of specialty if you are to get off to a fast start.

For those attracted to consulting, it is wise to remember that whatever knowledge you have to offer must somehow be sold. Success in this field rests squarely on your ability to attract and maintain clients.

Once you are established, many clients will come through referrals. However, the biggest reason for failure in consulting is that people don't foresee the personal selling effort required.

If selling is not your suit, but you are convinced you have a great deal to offer, you will have to attract one or more partners or employees who will devote their time to selling your services.

Some of the most popular consulting specialties include finance, marketing, new product development, data processing and systems, executive search and outplacement, cost reduction, and public relations.

There is also good activity in labor relations, electrical engineering, design, and other technical disciplines. If you want a consulting business, but do not have potential clients who will quickly retain you, then cash flow may be a problem. Allow time for getting started. Identify the organizations where what you know will be of greatest value. Later on, as your reputation grows, you can broaden your base.

If you would rather join an existing firm, there are thousands of consulting organizations that can benefit from timely addition of new talent. It is an easier way to get started than striking out on your own, and you can always benefit from the experience.

"General management consulting, EDP consulting, executive search and outplacement are good for many generalists. You need to be able to attract new business. Heavy phone contact and travel are drawbacks, but the pay can be good."

—*Bart Kellerher, HR Manager,*
Bell Atlantic

Regardless of the type of consulting you choose, remember that the special knowledge that makes a consultant valuable today may be obsolete several years later. So you need to allow time to keep current in your field. If you enjoy variety and intellectual challenge, then management consulting can be your right move.

(3) Do you have the ability to work as a personal producer?

Producers bring in business. Some examples include executive recruiters, financial planners, stockbrokers, real estate brokers, outplacement specialists, etc. If you have contacts and need a shift, this kind of role can be attractive. There are opportunities for producers in every discipline. The key is to focus on something you can do well.

(4) Are you able to start a new venture, buy a small firm or pursue investments?

Many executives have certain ideas and knowledge or have access to a facility that can provide the basis for a new venture. This direction offers the appeal of being your own boss, challenging your creativity and satisfying other needs during your career.

Perhaps you have an idea about a product around which you can develop a marketing or business plan. Can you put together financing beyond your own investment? This can be available from venture firms, private investors, or even some friends.

Many executives choose partnership options. Experience dictates that they work best when you choose someone whose skills complement your own or who has investment money to make a business grow. Purchasing smaller companies on an outright basis can offer unique advantages to those with an entrepreneurial instinct.

For example, there are opportunities that require involvement only to the extent you desire; these might include car washes, laundromats, theaters, apartments, parking lots, etc. You can put a personal stamp on such enterprises or stay in a passive role.

Specialty stores can also be candidates for purchase. Popular choices include hardware outlets, garden shops, nurseries, sporting goods stores and marinas, and product lines such as computers, men's clothing or even gourmet foods and wines. The possibilities could include small restaurants and inns, printing and travel services, manufacturing plants and numerous family businesses.

Investing, buying or selling is something that certain specialized executives also pursue. Obviously, this alternative requires an appropriate financial position and the knowledge of a particular area, or, at the very least, a willingness to learn.

Real estate investing has become an increasingly sophisticated field. The packages may involve vacant land, commercial buildings, single-or multiple-family residences, abandoned factories, government repossessions, etc. Active investors have earned millions, but there are no guarantees, and the risk can be high.

(5) Can you write or lecture commercially?

Writing with commercial opportunity in mind represents another option. Many people have aspired to write a book but never had time. Thousands of new authors make time as 40,000 new books are published every year.

A more important option for writers involves preparing articles that might be accepted by some of the country's 11,000-plus trade and business magazines.

The lecture circuit is open to individuals in the public eye. Agents can, for a percentage, arrange engagements that can reach or exceed $15,000 per lecture. Top rates are reserved for those with celebrity status.

However, thousands of people make an interesting career out of the lecture circuit. To get started, you will have to decide on timely or interesting subjects that are appropriate for you.

(6) Are you interested in managing a nonprofit or working in education?

Surprising to some, there are more than 20,000 trade organizations, and many are exceptionally well funded. Most trade associations are run like businesses and have similar needs.

On the administrative side, many executives have made major contributions in helping to keep educational institutions solvent. In many respects, education is like any other service business. People must be recruited and trained, and facilities must be operated efficiently. Information systems and data processing are needed; funds must be raised and public relations must be maintained.

"An increasing number of opportunities are available in our controversial, but challenging field of education. Relatively few business executives are aware of this."
—Mike McCall, Consultant,
Former Professor of Business

Those with corporate experience will find they are of particular value in the graduate schools of business. In fact, a number of universities have former corporate officers as professors, administrators, heads of development and fund-raising, and deans of their business schools.

Here, an advanced degree is usually a prerequisite. Those who favor classroom teaching or lecturing may still find that they eventually gravitate to management.

(7) What about serving on the boards of a few companies?

Many executives who can bring prestige and experience to smaller corporations become sought after for directorships. However, it usually takes some planning to get started. When you have served on one board, you will likely be invited to join others. That is particularly true if you have specific experience that will be apparent to nominating committees.

In fact, directorships on just three or four corporations, along with committee work, can often provide adequate income and lots of challenge. Among the largest firms, directors' fees recently averaged nearly $60,000 for 148 hours of work. The range of cash compensation runs from under $5,000 to $50,000. Total compensation can be two to four times higher as directors pay often includes an annual retainer, stock options, deferred compensation and expenses.

Some stock exchanges can direct you to clearinghouse services for executives interested in directorships. It is also possible to run a campaign aimed at existing directors, investment bankers, lawyers, and CEOs by discreetly inquiring whether your services might be valuable to one or more of the companies with which they are associated. Obviously, this avenue is most feasible for executives with strong reputations. However, even if this is not the case, it is possible to develop opportunities. Think carefully of what you have to offer that would set you apart.

If you are known as an executive who can increase productivity or cut costs, or if you have proven talents in securing financing, making acquisitions, or entering new markets, then it will be easy for many board members and CEOs to envision your contributions.

These openings are usually coordinated by the corporate secretary, who may be a good person to contact. Turnover tends to be at its peak in late winter and early spring, and a lengthy biography is a must. In cases like this, it is wise to decide on some limits as to how many companies you can help in this capacity. Because directorships now carry more exposure to liability, corporations no longer expect directors to serve for just a nominal sum or without proper insurance.

Are you entrepreneurial?

Many executives think they can make an easy transition to an entrepreneurial situation, but few achieve real success. To make sure you jump into this area with your eyes open, weigh your answers carefully to the following questions. Have you identified an area that you really like? Can you differentiate yourself from competition... do you have a special niche? Are you a hands on executive? Are you the type of person who can make decisions and move fast? Are you a good recruiter and motivator? Last, but not least, are you genuinely a resourceful type of person?

Summing Up

Many people view themselves solely by what they've done in the past. However, every month thousands of executives start new careers— areas in which they had no previous experience.

Of course, this is nothing new; as many historians have pointed out, Thomas Jefferson had more than eight different careers. More recently, Martin Luther King, Ronald Reagan, and scores of others have prospered by joining the ranks of notable career changers. Chances are there are several new careers that might be worth your examination.

—5—

How Do You
Expand Your Marketability?

When it comes to analyzing yourself, are you a straight-line thinker who has tunnel vision?

The new reality: To be competitive, you'll need more than a good executive background. So don't trap yourself by thinking, "This is simply who I am." The key is to capture everything about yourself that's marketable and then build an appeal beyond your obvious credentials. Six-figure job hunting is all about sales and marketing.

Are you thinking that your credentials are so strong, your resume so packed with achievements, that a good job will be yours for the asking? Maybe it should be that way, but our studies say something else.

Surprisingly, the "best-qualified" executives don't always make the "winner's circle." Who does? Those executives who do the best job of marketing their strengths, their skills—themselves.

If you are like most executives, you can increase your chances through a very simple point of view. It has been said time and again by psychologists, motivational speakers, spiritual leaders and coaches, that the most restrictive limits you face are those you put on yourself.

So, if you really want to be a serious candidate for a better position or a new career, don't put any limits on your thinking, at least not where your career possibilities are concerned.

Now, I believe that almost everyone's experience is more marketable than they realize. For whatever reason, most of us think of our experience in more narrow terms than we should. This type of thinking restricts our opportunities as many good situations pass by unnoticed.

In this discussion, we will review a number of ways to a broader view of your total experience and how you can describe it to potential employers.

"The best thing an executive can do today is to project his or her versatility. Executive jobs are being redefined—it's all about moving from one project to another and handling a lot of balls at one time."

—Ron Kessler,
Management Supervisor,
Advertising Agency

First, assume that all aspects of your knowledge are marketable. Make a list of things you know. For example, do you have knowledge of a job, a product, a process, or a market? It could come from work, hobbies, alumni relationships, reading or activities, or from suppliers, customers, friends, or your social life.

Your personality and character may also be more marketable than you think. Personality, of course, is just a word for that mysterious combination of traits that can either attract us to someone quite strongly, or on the other hand, leave us unimpressed.

More employment decisions are based on personality and chemistry than any other factor. It happens thousands of times every day. When it does, the employer is probably thinking something like this:

> *"He's certainly a professional... and positive and quick-thinking. I like him, and better yet, I trust him. He'll be able to get along with our executive team and provide leadership. I want him in this firm, and I'm going to make an offer right now."*

If most people seem to like you when they meet you, chances are you will meet people who have the power to offer you a position in a totally unrelated field.

Your interests and enthusiasm are also marketable. How many employers do you suppose have hired executives primarily because they showed a great deal of interest in their business? *The answer is, a lot!*

The opportunity you represent is marketable. If you can make an employer aware of an opportunity that you can help exploit, or a problem that you can help solve, you can actually create a job for yourself. Of course, if the employer is aware of the need or opportunity, all you need to do is let him know that you're the right person to handle it. (We'll talk more about this later.)

Can you describe your experience in ways that broaden your appeal?

Some executives at $100,000 and above view their previous jobs as having a narrow focus, and you may be thinking, *"I don't have a lot of options."* However, here is how you can expand your appeal and uncover more options.

Simply make a list of "any experience you've had" in a way that makes the experience more transferable.

First, list your experience by your skills and/or your duties that are commonly performed in almost all companies. Identifying your transferable skills is critical, for example, analyzing, organizing, group presentation skills, problem solving and so on.

In the current executive job market, employers are clearly placing a premium on executives who are versatile. The boundaries around many, if not most, executive jobs have changed as layers of management have been eliminated.

Executives who are perceived as being of the most potential value are men and women who can move from project to project handling a variety of assignments that draw upon different skills.

Because it is unrealistic for executives to think in terms of job security, the best way to protect yourself and your career is to be seen as a versatile team player capable of being a "money maker" in many different situations. In fact, it is a rare individual executive who can move ahead and stay ahead with a single predominant skill.

Second, list your experience according to various "business functions" that apply to most businesses, such as sales, production, accounting, marketing, human resources.

Third, list your experience by using "action verbs" that describe what you did and that translate those things into achievements. For example, *controlled, scheduled, wrote, improved, reshaped, built, created,* etc.

The simple fact is, the more ways you describe your experience, the more it can qualify you for jobs in many career fields and industries. That's because all organizations are basically involved in similar functions. So, before writing your resume, look at your experience from a few different slants, as I've indicated.

Fourth, you can also take a global view of your experience. This will help you expand the job market possibilities for yourself.

Can you communicate the
phrases that employers are looking for?

With the approach just described, you'll set the stage to build appeal beyond your factual credentials. However, you'll also need to design and follow your own communications plan... establishing and controlling how you want to be perceived.

Your need for this can best be appreciated by comparing it to the "platform" of a candidate for the presidency. The "platform" anticipates questions on major issues by formulating carefully-thought-out position statements to guide the candidate's answers.

Just like a political candidate, you can be perceived as better informed than the next person if you have taken the time to formulate your own communications strategy.

To do this, you must think through your assets, liabilities and goals, and arrive at a formula for guiding any communications about yourself. The strategy itself must be geared to maximizing your strengths and minimizing your liabilities.

Our philosophy revolves around identifying the "core" words and phrases that will be the heart of your communications strategy. This means that you want to be ready to use a series of words that communicate your special strengths.

These words should become a regular part of "your story" that you communicate to employers, recruiters, and others who might be of help. Please realize that regardless of your level, your "tickets alone" (advanced degrees, blue-chip background, lofty titles, etc.) will not necessarily motivate another employer to hire you in a six-figure position.

"My advice to any executive who wants to expand his or her marketability is to be able to give some examples of leadership. That's been a missing ingredient in our organization, and it's the one most desperately needed in other companies."

—VP HR,
Automotive Company

Those credentials offer only one form of reassurance that suggests you are right for the job. This is why you must use words that add interest beyond your credentials.

Now, as executives, when any of us recruit people, we usually have a concept in mind—a word description of the kind of person we are looking to hire. In the final analysis, we hire others for the traits, skills, and abilities that certain key descriptive words and phrases imply.

Decide on some phrases that relate to you, and select those that set you apart from people who are competing with you. For example, you may have *"operated effectively under pressure."* Perhaps you are *"an excellent motivator,"* or you may have *"built highly effective teams."*

Most executives can make a list of at least 30 key words and concepts. Used appropriately, these words and conepts can set you apart from competition and convey the unique advantages you have to offer. Here is a small sample of the key traits that employers may be looking for:

> *Entrepreneurial strengths; experience in a growth company; resourceful problem-solver; intuitive decision-maker; experienced in formulating policy; ability to get things done and inspire others to better performance; have previously initiated sweeping changes; performed against tight deadlines; built profits in international operations; and so on.*

Much has been written in recent years about America's search for executive leadership at all levels of business and government. And if there is one quality you want to be able to communicate, then leadership ability is it. But just how is leadership projected, especially if you're not a celebrity in the business world?

An article that appeared in United Airlines' in-flight magazine examined the qualities necessary to be perceived as a leader in today's environment. The observations included much of the following:

Most experts say that real leaders possess and communicate real convictions. These are seen as strong feelings and principles that have grown with them over time. Obviously, those convictions need to match the requirements of the organization and those who might follow.

Whether it's justified or not, leadership is also attributed to executives who create an image of operating at the far edge of the frontier—where new products and solutions are being planned for the future.

We tend to think of leaders as those who have vision and who have the ability to develop new things or bring the best improvements to older ones. Other attributes that people ascribe to leaders are that they are creative, intuitive and passionate, and that they project integrity, trust, and boldness.

Put all of these traits together, and they represent most of the criteria that contribute to people being viewed as charismatic. Naturally image, attitude, appearance, and presence are all important factors, and we will discuss these characteristics later on in our review of interviewing for executive positions.

Can you develop some "stories" to give your experience more impact?

Most executives who interview you will often forget what you said in a matter of minutes. To ensure that your points are both memorable and credible, use a technique for creating interesting "stories."

SODAR is an acronym that stands for Situation, Opportunities, Duties, Actions, and Results. It represents a process of describing your past experience in a way that resembles a motion picture. Here's how you can use it:

❑ Situation. Explain a job you held by first describing the situation when you began employment. This enables you to provide some interesting background information, e.g., what had been taking place when you arrived.

❑ Opportunities. Then bring up information about the opportunities that the job presented to you, the group you were part of, and the firm.

❑ Duties. Subsequently, you describe your duties.

❑ Actions. However, more importantly, your emphasis should quickly move to those actions taken by you and other members of your team.

❑ Results. And then relate what results occurred.

SODAR means "telling the whole story." If it's well told, it will generate more genuine interest than any recitation of duties or responsibilities. Furthermore, it will help people remember you ahead of others.

Of course, the R in SODAR (results) is the most important. Try to quantify the results. For example, you cut costs by $100,000 or 20%. Remember, don't be modest.

"Many executives have told us that it was their use of carefully rehearsed stories that most impressed people and won offers for them. This is hardly unexpected. Anyone who has listened to a speech or a sales presentation knows how much more interesting it is if the speaker uses short stories to demonstrate a point."

—Michele Lutz, President, Princeton/Masters Client Services

In many administrative functions, it is not easy to quantify. In these cases, measure results using statements like, *"I did it in half the time,"* or *"The system I developed was adopted throughout the company,"* or *"I won an award"* etc.

Try to describe results in terms of dollars, percent increases, or units. Indicate any good things you did to help your organizations and how you took on extra tasks. Describe how you helped your superiors achieve their goals and also the results they achieved.

Develop stories that cover situations where you can demonstrate the value of fresh thinking as a means to improve productivity or show that you have solved a wide variety of problems in diverse areas.

Now, let's recap the primary ways you can expand your marketability. First, broaden your appeal by writing out your experience according to (a) business functions, (b) your skills and duties, and (c) your achievements.

Second, because your knowledge and interests are marketable, list all the things you know and any special interests that might appeal to employers.

Remember that your personality, character, and enthusiasm are marketable. The opportunity you represent is also marketable; list problems you can help an employer solve. Once you have uncovered what's marketable about yourself, plan on building your appeal beyond your credentials by making use of a "communications plan."

Start by identifying words that reflect your special strengths. Then identify the key phrases that describe your traits, skills and abilities that employers look for. Use them in all your written and verbal communications; however, to make your experiences more interesting and memorable, incorporate them with the story-telling concept I've described.

How much will your age affect your marketability?

As American business has been getting leaner over the last decade, there has been a noticeable trend towards the hiring of younger executives. As businesses and companies have been re-engineered, many six-figure executives in their 50s and early 60s have seen their jobs eliminated or they have been replaced.

A quick look at the 1994 Annual Report issued by PepsiCo, Inc., gives perhaps a good example of the trend that has been taking place. In this report, they listd the chief executive officers of their major divisions and their ages. Here's what they published:

CEO of Pepsi Cola, North America .... age 49
CEO of Frito Lay, Inc. .... age 46
CEO of PepsiCo Foods / Beverages, Int.. age 44
CEO of Pizza Hut, Inc. .... age 51
CEO of Taco Bell Corp. .... age 49
CEO of Kentucky Fried Chicken. .... age 42
CEO of PepsiCo Restaurants, Int. .... age 42
CEO of PepsiCo Food Systems. .... age 46
CEO of PepsiCo Worldwide Rest's. .... age 50

The same report listed 36 corporate officers of PepsiCo, Inc. The median age of this group was 47. Of those, 8 were in their 30s, 14 were in their 40s, 12 were in their 50s, and 2 were 60 or more. The CEO of PepsiCo was listed as 59.

"If you're currently in your 50s or older, the key points of advice are as follows: First, you may need to run a campaign that is broader and that focuses you on exploring more career and industry options. Second, you'll need to make an extra effort to run a first-rate professional search. Third, you'll need to be more aggressive in placing your credentials, making far more contacts than you might expect."

—Tom Smith, President
Managing Director, Princeton/Masters
Northern California Operations

Summing Up

Start thinking about yourself in the broadest possible terms. Examine everything about your experience, your knowledge, your skills, and the functions with which you've been involved. When it comes to a six-figure job search, you can never limit your view of yourself, and you must build appeal beyond your credentials.

— 6 —

Is There One Major Rule
for Getting the Right Interviews?

Would you rather proceed by trial and error, trusting to fate? Or would you rather let your actions be guided by a strategic plan?

The new reality: Job hunting is a numbers game, and multiple contacts are a prerequisite to getting multiple calls, interviews, and offers. Above $100,000, taking the time to think through a plan will save you a great deal of time, money, and trial and error.

The following discussion can be the basis for doing in a compressed time segment what most executives take six to 12 months to accomplish.

Your starting point is to look at job hunting in an entirely new way. This means investing in a simple insurance policy for success, one that I call a personal action plan. It will enable you to job hunt with far less strain, confusion or worry, and keep you on track.

The very idea of an action plan was practically unknown a decade ago. Today, however, it makes a lot of sense for any executive who is entering the job market. Having a plan will help you take job-hunting actions systematically and will produce far better results.

The concept is simple. There are no gimmicks involved, and you don't need to forecast the future. Rather, it is a process for deciding on job-hunting actions, then following through in a way that will bring you a greater number of interviews at the right level.

Without a plan, chances are you will spend too much energy on haphazard actions, trusting to fate that you'll get the results you want. Planning, on the other hand, brings focus to your efforts and sets the stage for you to control your actions as well as your destiny in the job market.

"The less-aggressive executive job seeker has a disadvantage of major proportions. Aggressiveness equals getting discovered."
— *Ralph Dieckman,*
Executive Recruiter

Being organized will also help you overcome rejection, stay on the right track, and remain goal-oriented. In short, action plans play a key role for job seekers, just as marketing plans do for companies.

For the purposes of this discussion, we'll assume that you will settle on your career and industry directions and financial goals. At this point, therefore, I want to focus on how you should plan actions that will develop interviews.

As you approach your plan, you will need to first decide on the priority you will give your campaign. If you are out of work, severely underemployed, or about to relocate, then it should receive top priority. If this happens to be your situation, design an aggressive campaign—one that can potentially produce more activity than you really need.

On the other hand, if you are currently employed and working 60 hours a week, you may wish to design a campaign plan over a longer period.

Any plan requires a timetable. For most six-figure executives, we recommend an effort that will last 16 weeks. If it ends up taking a little longer, that's okay, but start by thinking that you want to reach your goal within this period.

You should also realize that experience has indicated that to end up choosing between several offers, you'll need to gear your action plan to generate 15 or more interview opportunities.

What are the key elements that are critical in any marketing effort?

Consider for a moment how products are successfully sold. In most cases, a marketing plan is followed.

The starting point is to <u>bring to the surface</u> all of the vital product information. As I've already discussed, you've got to dig deep to understand what you have to offer the market.

Next, each product must be <u>positioned</u> correctly. In your case, you have to know which potential buyers you will appeal to and in what capacity. You seldom see a product that claims it can do anything for anyone.

Then, you must be willing to <u>promote</u> your product. For executive job hunting, you need to decide what you want to communicate, and then draft all resumes and letters.

Of course, products need be <u>priced</u> as high as possible... as long as they sell. While your income potential will ultimately be determined by supply and demand, your marketing and negotiation strategy can make a difference.

When a product is ready to go, it needs to reach the market with the right <u>distribution</u>. You will need to decide on how you will get your message out, and where it will go? Will you go directly to employers or through recruiters, friends, and other contacts or both?

As you go through your job search, why not take stock of your progress?

Are you keeping up with a plan? Are you getting positive feedback on your materials? Are your goals realistic? Is it time for some fine-tuning or adjustments?

If you don't see yourself zeroing in on the right offer, commit to another period of active campaigning that follows the same approach, or modify your plan.

"Executives just can't expect to go out and find another six-figure job. This is a pure sales process. They need to differentiate themselves from all the other job-seekers out there, and they need to do it with a great many employers."

—Glen Scott, EVP
Princeton/Masters
Northern California Operations

Now, you may be close to an offer, or you may not have made much progress, in which case you'll need to reaffirm commitment to a campaign philosophy with a "whatever it takes" attitude. As long as your goal remains unchanged and you remain committed to reaching it, determination is the key that will ultimately get you there.

As I said, executive job hunting is a numbers game. The more good contacts you make, the more good opportunities will come your way. In the chapters that follow, we'll be discussing each of the avenues in which you should plan activity

Summing Up

In today's competitive market, you will never get enough interviews if you operate by trial and error. Develop a plan that is carefully strategized and easy to follow. Make sure that it addresses what you should do, week by week. Do it right, and the net result will be that you'll get the right new job in less than half the time.

— 7 —

What Is the Fastest Way for Finding Leads to New Jobs?

Are you going to sit back and wait for leads to come your way, or do you want leads now?

The new reality: Every day you must be looking for that piece of news that will be the lead you need. Your ability to recognize and go after opportunity is crucial.

*T*he following discussion is especially important for executives who want to change careers or industries.

Why are over 90% of all six-figure jobs filled privately, and how do companies do this? Well, they seek to fill openings privately because it has proven to be an effective and less expensive method for finding quality executives. Many companies cannot afford to retain an executive search firm and may simply look at resumes they've kept on file.

However, most firms will ultimately fill positions through personal referrals or by hiring someone who simply contacts them at the right time. By hiring in this manner, they avoid the costs of recruiter fees and advertising expenses.

Now, if you can learn where these openings exist, it stands to reason that you can have a major edge over your competitors. What's more, you might be able to have your credentials up for singular consideration, instead of applying right along with scores of others.

How do you learn of six-figure job openings that are not advertised or listed with recruiters?

To find employers with unadvertised openings, all you need to do is follow events in the press. We call those situations Emerging Opportunities. Of course, you can also uncover jobs that are not advertised, through mailings, telemarketing, and networking, but following events in the press is the most direct way.

"We're in the telecommunications business, and our industry is in real flux. We go outside for talent and have hired from areas as diverse as orange juice and fashion. Naturally, I prefer industry people, but it's all a matter of who comes to our attention at the right time."

—Marketing VP,
Telecommunications Company

Events occur every day, in thousands of firms that ultimately lead senior executives to begin the process of privately looking for new people. These events are often reported in local and national business publications, trade magazines, newsletters and newspapers. Here you will find articles on growth situations, new divisions, new facilities, new products, reorganizations, acquisitions, high-level executive changes and plans for investments or expansion.

For companies undergoing these transitions, chances are they will need to attract good people to handle problems or capitalize on their opportunities. The activity in these companies won't usually be limited to one or two functions either. They can be expected to need people in all functional categories—sales, marketing, finance, etc.

While private openings are being filled by all types of employers, they are filled with far greater frequency in organizations experiencing significant change.

Using news events to find opportunities has been the key to success for people at all levels and from all occupations. Here's how a few executives have capitalized by uncovering openings through events:

> *A financial executive learned that a troubled manufacturer was divesting a division to raise cash. He called the new president and arranged to meet him and explain how he might help. Four weeks later, he became the CFO of this company.*
>
> *A marketing manager read that a European corporation had bought a local company. He wrote to express interest and suggested a dialogue when European officials visited there. Twelve weeks later, he was VP-Marketing, U.S.A., at $120,000.*
>
> *An ambitious sales executive read that a competitor recently acquired two competitors in his field. Sensing that this would create a new need for high-powered sales executives, he placed a call and four weeks later was offered a six-figure position.*

Can you take advantage
of organizational change when you see it?

When you read about a company that is giving off signals that they may be hiring at an above-average rate, don't stop at the obvious implications. Use what we refer to as "ripple-effect thinking." This is simply taking the time to think about all of the changes that may be occurring in the company—up and down the line and across many functions.

> *"Executive job hunting is all about one thing. Access to information is the name of the game. "*
>
> *—Roger Iverson, Former VP HR, Division of American Cyanamid*

You may also get some good ideas about using information that you read about one company to find opportunities with a company's suppliers, customers, and even their competitors. To take full advantage of emerging opportunities, consider the following example:

You read that a manufacturer is starting a division to sell a new kind of packaging for protecting sensitive health-care supplies. The obvious implications are that this company could very well need people in marketing and sales. Because it's a new division, you might also expect that there will be some need for finance people as well.

If you're a packaging engineer, you might also project a need for that capability to support the sales effort. Those possibilities would be real enough, but now let's use "ripple-effect thinking" to see if we can infer some other needs.

If you're an engineer with knowledge in this product area, you know this concept will concern competitors. You might contact them to help in the new product area.

Or, you may be someone who is experienced in dealing with regulatory authorities. You recognize that the potential customers for this product will have to deal with these authorities to gain product approval. Consequently, this firm might need someone like you to take charge of regulatory matters.

Going even further, consider the case of an executive who had been an executive director with a charity. For a number of reasons, he wanted to make a move to the corporate sector. "Ripple-effect thinking" helped him to uncover a number of attractive possibilities.

He learned that a major corporation was expanding its nuclear facilities. He reasoned that the company would have to deal with community groups opposing these facilities. Given his experience in community affairs and controversial subjects, he wrote the company about whether they might have an opening for someone to fill that need.

What about organizations with problems?

Problems often imply one of two things: managers in certain functions haven't been performing well, or the company needs to develop new capabilities in order to survive and grow. Organizations with problems often need help from the following types of people:

> *marketing people who can identify new markets and launch new products; financial executives who can cut costs or raise capital; general managers who can take responsibility for plant closings; COOs who can supply new leadership; human resource executives who can help find all these other people.*

Most of the time a CEO or a board member will be the logical person for you to contact. Keep in mind that many employers undergoing change are actually the smaller and faster-growing firms, and they are far less constrained by hiring traditions common to major companies.

Organizations that are on a fast track will usually be looking for executives with the best natural ability and who have enthusiasm, dedication and the right work ethic.

Summing Up

It's often been said that information is power, and that's exactly what news of emerging opportunities provides. The ability to recognize and go after leads has been the key to success for many executives. Make it part of your ongoing routine to use this proven lead-sourcing method.

— 8 —

How Do You Make the Most of Executive Recruiters?

Are you among the group of executives who assume that their relationships with recruiters will be all they need?

The new reality: The chance of an executive recruiter filling a job that is right for you, at the moment you contact them is remarkably small... and getting smaller all the time. If you are not well known in your field, blanketing the recruiter market is the only strategic way to go.

*T*here's no question that recruiters can be of help to your career. But, if you have to send them a resume, the chance of them working on a job that is just right for you at the moment you contact them is very small. However, you can improve your odds by using superior materials and by contacting large numbers of recruiters.

Executive search firms typically fill positions from $70,000 to $300,000 and up. Many people refer to them as headhunters, and their assignment is to find qualified candidates who meet highly specialized criteria.

Retained for searches on an exclusive basis, most of these firms charge their employer clients 30% to 33% of the annual compensation of the position they are seeking to fill. To distinguish themselves within their industry, they are also sometimes referred to as "retainer recruiters."

The number of six-figure job openings they control is sizable, but still only 9% of the market. Furthermore, on a national scale, fewer than a dozen firms control the majority of the business, even though there are upwards of 800 organizations that claim to be active in the field.

> *"We review every resume, but the background of the candidate must be right on target for what we're working on. Otherwise, there's not a chance we'll respond."*
> *—Doug Andrews, Executive Recruiter, Clarey and Andrews*

Certain recruiters enjoy considerable prestige, often working only on select high-level assignments. However, there are also many very fine smaller firms who specialize in just a single industry or several industries or disciplines.

On a personal level, recruiters are usually articulate professionals who have a broad knowledge of business. The successful people in the field are generally excellent marketing executives themselves.

How do executive recruiters find candidates? Recruiters have a preference for achievers, people who make strong first impressions and who are successfully employed in other firms. These are the individuals who are most presentable to their clients and who are easiest to sell to them.

Their sources for finding people range from directories and articles in the press to their own broad-range contacts and files of resumes.

Of course, the preferred relationships with these firms are the ones that begin with their contacting you. Being visible in your industry is the major key to success with recruiters. Being in a hot field or industry can improve things still further.

How do you make
contact with the right recruiters?

If you have kept track of the recruiters who have called you in the past, one of the first things you should now do is renew these relationships.

There are also many directories available who provide listings of most of the nation's executive recruiters. Most outplacement firms also acquire databases and supplement them with their own research.

To get results through a mail campaign, you are going to have to send them a superior summary of your qualifications. At the six-figure level, mailings of 300 or more are common, and should go out at the beginning of your search. Keep in mind that recruiters are "assignment-oriented." They will be focused on filling their active contracts. In most cases, all that will happen is that you will simply be getting into their files.

Keep records of all replies from recruiters. Using impressive materials, over a six week period you can expect positive response that will usually range from 1% to 4%—depending on your field, industry, and income level.

If your correspondence fails to supply a phone number that is answered during normal business hours, you will lose many leads. Voice-mail service or an answering machine is a must. Another point to remember is that a second mailing to the same list three months later usually produces equal results.

"Ever since the late 1980s, we've been inundated with unsolicited resumes. On the average, I would say our largest office receives 200 or more each day."
—*Duke Foster, Managing Director, Korn/Ferry International, Stamford, CT.*

Keep in mind that many large firms are contacted by 50 to 200 job seekers each day. This means there will be instances where a recruiter calls you *months* after the firm first receives your resume.

Regardless, recruiters will be interested primarily in those viewed as marketable, who have blue-chip or high-demand backgrounds, and who have industry knowledge that can quickly help their clients.

You will be most popular with executive recruiters if you are a person who will explore more attractive situations but who is not too unhappy with his or her current employer. Be honest while pursuing a soft sell. If you are desperate or too available, they will never recommend you to their clients.

One last thought on recruiters. In an interview with Duke Foster of *Korn/Ferry*, often considered the largest search firm with 58 offices worldwide, he indicated that every executive resume they receive is scanned. However, in most cases, if there is no indication of current income or range of desired earnings, your material will never find it's way into their national and international database which is maintained in Los Angeles. At the six-figure level this is good advice where all recruiters are concerned.

And, by the way, when you visit them, you had better be good at interviewing or you may have to write a firm off for the balance of your career. Remember, the recruiter is simply measuring how well you are qualified... and how well you will sell.

Summing Up

Executive recruiters can be very important; however, many people depend far too much on them, and the job search becomes a long waiting game. Others get discouraged about their marketability and draw negative conclusions about their chances.

Cover the market with a mass mailing utilizing superior materials, and consider doing a follow-up mailing 12 weeks later. However, don't allow more than 10% of your job search effort to be focused on recruiters.

— 9 —

Is Answering
Ads Worth Your Time?

*Do you rush to get the Sunday classifieds or
The Wall Street Journal ads?*

*The new reality: Less than 1% of all six-fig-
ure jobs are ever advertised, and the percentage declines every year. However, there are a
few angles that can help increase your odds.*

*M*ost estimates place the advertised portion of the six-
figure job market at less than 1% of all openings that get
filled. What's more, many of the more attractive advertised openings bring 100, 200 or even 400 responses. Ads
that attract up to 1,000 candidates are not that unusual.
This clearly makes answering ads the most competitive
area you can tackle.

To make things worse, many executives answer ads
without giving any strategic thought to how to gain a
competitive advantage. They also use resumes that are
average in appearance, disclose far too many liabilities
and fail to highlight why the person can fill the position.
Rarely interesting or imaginative, they are simply lost
among the overwhelming numbers of other candidates.

When you start your search, answer all good ads from
the last 13 weeks. A certain percentage of those openings
will already be filled, but just as surely a number will still

be open. In some fields, the openings you uncover this way can be quite large.

> *"I never found a job by answering an ad or going through a recruiter. I landed my present position by meeting the president of the company at a golf tournament."*
>
> *—Don Cockroft,*
> *Senior VP, Northcoast Energy,*
> *Former NFL All-Pro–Cleveland Browns*

As you identify new advertisements to answer, it is usually advisable to delay your response five days, to minimize the risk of not making the first cut. When employers screen a lot of applicants, they begin by discarding any resumes that include anything that will rule the person out. This produces a manageable amount of paperwork, which is then reviewed more carefully.

If you respond five days after the ad appears, rather than when the employer was inundated with paper, your chances of getting a good reading go up dramatically.

By the way, did you ever see an ad and feel, *that describes me exactly?* Well, as a general rule, after you have responded, if you have not heard anything after two weeks have passed, you should follow up.

If you were a good fit for the job, answering ads twice can work. Very few of your competitors will do this, and all employers give a big edge to people who really want to be with them.

Are you willing to use some creative approaches when answering ads?

Another strategy that has worked for a number of executives involves the use of what is called downgrading, upgrading and sidegrading.

For example, a company advertising for a CFO might be willing to hire a senior financial type who could move up to CFO. It isn't so much the title they are after, as the skills and talent. That's an example of downgrading.

By the same token, a company advertising for a Director of Manufacturing might be persuaded to hire a VP of Manufacturing, provided someone could persuade the potential employer that such a move would be cost efficient and would offer added capabilities. That's an upgrade.

Ads can also be used as signals of private openings in other areas of the company. If you see a company hiring a number of salespeople, that's a fairly reliable indicator that they are also hiring a few executives in other areas.

As you probably noticed, employers who land large contracts or who are introducing hot new products tend to go through aggressive recruiting in cycles.

How do you get more interviews when you answer ads?

The answer to this question is quite simple: Wherever possible, always use letters rather than resumes.

As I mentioned, because employers receive so many resumes, they tend to start by screening out non-qualifiers. This is a critical point. Because resumes provide more facts, they can work against you in some situations.

"When I was at Rubbermaid, we did a fair amount of advertising. If you're an executive who is answering ads, I'd say the whole key is to make sure your letter is customized to the requirements."

—Clifford Van Dyck,
Van Dyck, Petrie and McCombs

Make use of strong letters, ones that are targeted at the requirements for success in the position. Of course, there are situations where it is wise to use a resume with a cover letter; however, your resume needs to be right on target for the opening that is advertised.

Summing Up

If you rely on answering ads, you can get very discouraged about your marketability. Uncovering ads should receive less than one-twentieth of your job hunting efforts! To enjoy success at marketing yourself, you need to be creative, you need to get out of your routine, and you need to start using new avenues to find the job you really want.

— 10 —

Are You Ready to Maximize
Your Direct Mail Opportunity?

*Are you hesitant about launching a profes-
sional direct mail campaign? Have you been
the "few letters a day" type waiting for the
phone to ring?*

*The new reality: If you know what you're do-
ing, direct-mail marketing, combined with
proper telemarketing, can be a predictable
way to success; however, never assume it can
be done with small numbers or run-of-the-mill
materials.*

Some people will tell you that direct mail marketing
doesn't work. However, they probably did a job search
without understanding that direct marketing is the most
scientific area of sales and marketing and without having
the benefit of the advice just discussed.

If you distribute cheap-looking materials, send standard junk mail resumes and form letters, and use the
wrong list, you will be wasting your time.

I'm often amused by executives who say that direct-
mail marketing doesn't work. You've seen horror stories
about unemployed executives who have sent out 5,000
resumes—who have yet to get an interview—and, therefore, things are really tough out there!

However, most executives can achieve far more with direct mail than they thought possible. It takes excellent writing, the right targets, telephone follow-up and adherence to proven rules of direct mail. But considering that your career is at stake, it's worth it.

"What would I do if I had to look for a job? Well, besides exhausting my contacts, and covering recruiters, I'd get out an awful lot of resumes and letters to board members who might view me as a possibility— and that's regardless of location. Please don't quote me, I'm not seeking a new job."
—CEO, High Tech Company

Every day we are all on the receiving end of direct mail. However bad that junk mail may look to you, the fact is that the ones you see again and again are working; otherwise, the senders wouldn't be wasting money by repeating the process.

Direct mail is a game of testing, revising, and testing some more, until you get the right return for the right dollars. And perhaps the number-one rule in direct mail is that "long copy is the name of the game," because that's what it takes to motivate all of us to action from *unasked-for correspondence.*

Why? Well, give it a little thought. Let's assume your local lawn mower shop wants you to come in and see a new product they're carrying.

Assume that you and your next door neighbor are both out cutting your lawns on a brutally hot day. However, your lawn mower keeps sputtering and coughing, stopping and starting, and finally it passes out completely.

Then, the postman arrives at both residences with this long piece of junk mail that tells you all about a revolutionary new lawn mower, a long explanation of why it's superior to everything else ever manufactured and guess what, it's available locally.

Now, chances are your neighbor will look at the mailing piece for about two seconds and toss it, wondering how anyone could ever read all that material.

Obviously, he isn't in the market for a lawn mower. On the other hand, because the mailing piece has reached you at precisely the right time, you are apt to read it quite thoroughly. Perhaps you might be motivated to make a local visit and a purchase!

Now, your position, relative to using direct mail is really very similar. Your interest is in reaching the right person who might be in the market for someone like you right now. No one else counts.

Direct mail and telemarketing have to work together to produce the optimum results. For small custom mailings, I would go for a handwritten envelope marked "private and confidential," sent with a regular postage stamp.

By the way, the job of the letter itself would not only be to produce an interview, but to pre-sell you. Then, when you meet, hopefully the process has been moved downstream a step.

What are the chances? Well, it's a low percentage game. However, if you have the right targets and a good story, then those few you reach who are in the market for someone like you are going to want to read about you. After all, they have a problem to be solved or an opportunity on which to capitalize!

To make direct mail work, you will also need to understand how to use telemarketing in conjunction with direct mail.

Of course, very few employers will be needing someone like you the day your letter arrives. The key is to follow traditional direct marketing and follow-up techniques. Here are some initial thoughts for you to consider.

"Unless one thing happens, I don't think direct mail is worth anything. You better have the right people to get in touch with or you'll come up with zero."

—Sam Robertson,
VP HR, Computer Company

Direct-mail marketing works well because you can project your best image, avoid initial disclosure of any liabilities, and make contact that is free from competition.

What's more, you have a universe of possibilities to contact. This method for generating interviews also offers the best potential for helping you change careers or land a position at a major increase in earnings.

Can you identify the right employers to contact and decide on your priority list?

Start by drawing up a selective list of preferred organizations and people in them to contact. Your "priority list" needs to be developed according to the industries for whch you are best suited, and your preferred locations.

In the largest organizations, CEOs or senior vice presidents in charge of specific functions are recommended targets. In smaller firms you will need to reach the top executive or owner.

Your next step is to divide your initial list into three parts by identifying your "best of best," other "prime choices," and those who are really "secondary choices" you might consider.

This carefully tailored target list of employers should be added to as you go through your search. Your goal, of course, is to get an interview with the right person in these organizations.

To make it easy to do this, you must take advantage of the expanding world of computer databases to create your priority list. Literally dozens of databases are available, any of which can save you time and enable you to quickly launch your direct-mail and telemarketing efforts.

In some cases, you can purchase a floppy disc or CD-ROM from associations on a specific industry, from chambers of commerce, or from business periodicals.

Keep in mind that all of them will be at least 10% out of date. Typically, you can select organizations by industry, location and size and then print out information such as the company name and address, telephone number, names of CEOs and their officers by area of specialty.

Can you design a small "custom" mailing to the best of your priority list?

Your initial step should involve sending a highly customized marketing letter directed toward a small number of companies that are your very best prospects.

Depending on the size of your list, this effort might be restricted to your "best of best." Typically, you are talking here about no more than 15% to 20% of your entire priority list.

Here, you must communicate something in your letter that also customizes your approach to these employers. In essence, within a standard letter you need to insert a few thoughts that create a more tailored marketing approach.

"I look at resumes that cross my desk. If something stands out as a fit to the needs that I have at the moment, I may respond directly. It's a matter of timing; otherwise I pass them on to HR."

—Jim Falletti, Senior VP,
Ameritech Corp.

You'll need to spread your mailing out over a period of time, so you can afford to personally call everyone you have written. For most senior executives, a plan for at least 300 or more custom mailings is usually recommended. As a general rule, two-page letters (without a resume attached) produce the best results.

Next, can you do a large-scale mailing to your remaining priority list?

The second step of your plan should call for mailings to your remaining possibilities. I call it your "macro" mailing. The assumption is that among the careful list you have put together, there is a demand for your talents, and a small percentage will probably be looking for someone like you either right now or over the next few months.

Here, a superior presentation of your background and what you can do for the company are key. For those with highly marketable backgrounds, your large mailing effort alone may generate more than enough interview activity. If it doesn't produce, it probably means that your materials were off-base or your background and list selection did not fit.

Now, the higher your income requirements, the larger the effort required. Everything depends on proper targets and truly superior materials.

There are certain specialties in which job seekers have a limited number of potential employers, for example musicians, educators, broadcasters, etc. Here, your campaign will be most effective with long-copy letters.

For most executives, a secondary mailing of 1,000 or more is usually recommended. This "macro marketing" effort can include the last two levels of your priority list.

Typically, you should use a cover letter and a two-page resume, or a two-page letter that could be adjusted for different industries. Mailings in waves will again allow time for selected telephone follow-up. For executives who are marketable on a national scale, mailings of 3,500 are not uncommon.

What types of correspondence
work best in a direct mail campaign?

Letters can be more important than resumes. You must customize your appeal for each audience, even if you need to design up to a dozen types of specialty letters.

Typically, different letters should be used for answering ads, sending to HR executives, contacting CEOs, answering opportunities uncovered through events, networking friends, networking influentials, for requesting references, and for contacting recruiters.

Cover letters should be interesting and brief. Get to the point and make sure it's good.

Letter resumes are stand-alone letters that are not forwarded with a resume. They should provide sufficient "resume-type information" to stimulate interest. Use them whenever you want to fully tailor the description of your credentials, and avoid revealing any liabilities.

"Third-party letters can be very effective if the right person is writing for you. The person doesn't need to be a close friend; just make it easy for them to assist. I'd prepare a letter for their signature."

—John Thomas Windsor,
Former HR Executive, Hoechst Celanese

Handwritten memos are fast and easy to send off, and executives are used to such notes. If you have a superior resume that is on target for your audience, attaching such notes can work very well.

Obviously, the content of your letters will be critically important. Materials that emphasize what you can do, as well as the results you can bring, are ideal.

Next best are letters that talk about your previous accomplishments and the results you achieved. Least effective are letters that list your past experience and work history.

If you write your own letters, there are some basic requirements. Some people start without a clear picture of what they intend to say, then get caught up in telling their story and wind up with a highly disorganized letter. To avoid this trap, the opening should demonstrate your specific interest (knowledge of the firm, its industry, etc.) and explain your reason for writing.

The body must convey your qualifications and potential benefits. Lead off with your best selling-points. Enlarge upon them, citing examples when appropriate, and present yourself as the answer to a need or problem. The closing should be straightforward. It should restate your interest, confirm your desire for an interview and say when you will be following up.

Isn't it just common sense that your success will depend on your list, your materials, your phone skills and your approach?

Let's assume you were seeking a Vice President of Sales position. Here are some of the direct-mail approaches you might consider taking.

High risk. Sent randomly to CEOs. Doesn't work.

Slightly better. Sent to people by generic titles, e.g. all SVPs of Sales at Fortune 500 firms. May result in no response. Takes great credentials to work.

Much better. Sent to SVP Sales, by name, selected by industry, size, and location. Can be very good with follow-up.

Very good. Sent to SVP Sales by name, in industries where you have experience, mention it early and follow up.

Excellent. Sent to SVP Sales to whom you have spoken. Great if you can get your telemarketing on a roll.

Also Excellent. Sent to SVP Sales, by name, where mailing goes out under someone else's letterhead.

Outstanding. Sent to SVP Sales, by name, to whom you've been referred by someone, with telephone follow-up.

Best. Sent to SVP Sales, by name, whom you have met socially or in business, with follow-up.

Can you stick to some proven direct-marketing rules? Here they are.

Direct mail is a separate marketing specialty. What works and what doesn't has already been proven! If you stick to some basic direct-marketing rules, you can dramatically lift your chances for success. Here are the basics:

- ❏ Assembly-line materials don't work.

- ❏ Long copy works best, but letters must be crisp. Keep sentences short. Avoid flowery words. Keep paragraphs to five or six lines. Indent the first line.

- ❏ If you have industry experience, mention it early!

- ❏ Use the names of both the firm and the individual in the body of your letter.

- ❏ In most cases don't explain why you are looking.

- ❏ Persuasive letters "read" just like you "speak." Read your letters out loud to see if they need more work.

- ❏ Personalize your letters by using "I," "my," or "we."

- ❏ Always be enthusiastic. Everyone prefers people who really want to be associated with him/her.

- ❏ Commit yourself to a telephone follow-up. Name the date and general time you will call.

- ❏ Never mention your expected income.

- ❏ Keep records of all direct mail. Follow-up mailings get 80% of the response of your first mailing.

- ❏ If you have a strong interest in a large firm, consider sending materials to several top executives in that organization.

- ❏ Use a standard of quality in your materials that is befitting a six-figure executive. Cheap-looking material doesn't work at your level.

What response can you expect from your direct mail effort?

The lower your position objectives, the higher the response you can expect from your mailing. Above the $100,000 level, a 0.5% positive response is good.

"I sent out 1,100 letters along with my resume. I had 14 interview opportunities and received two attractive offers."

—CFO, $100,000,000 Company

"I did 150 custom mailings and got four interviews. Then I did a mass mailing of 3,700 and got 17 opportunities for interviews. Over 11 weeks I was interviewed for 13 situations and received 3 offers."

—Formerly Unemployed $175,000 Manufacturing Executive

Positive response refers to any favorable inquiry over a four to six week period. It may be a request for further information, a phone discussion or a request for an interview. For example, assume you presently earn $125,000 and that you have done a mailing to 1,000 firms within a couple of hours of where you live.

If over a period of four to six weeks, and as a result of both your marketing and follow-up, eight to 12 firms (.8 to 1.2%) express an interest in a meeting, you will have done well. Remember, these will be your best possible leads—where employers are responding with a specific need in mind right now. Effective use of the phone is the key to achieving any dramatic improvement in these statistics.

Here is an example of a campaign that was based solely on direct mail. It involved two men simultaneously—

the EVP and number-two man in a pharmaceutical firm and the president of a division of the same firm. Both were terminated because of a merger. The EVP was moved into a presidency with a division of another pharmaceutical firm in New York inside of ten weeks. Fewer than 80 three-page custom letters were circulated within the industry—each of which was followed up.

The other executive campaigned for 18 weeks before relocating as CEO of a smaller west coast firm. Fifteen hundred letters were involved, and we made use of two different three-page biographies.

Another example involved the CEO of a Fortune 500 firm who was ousted by his board. Here, we launched a third-party direct mail and telemarketing effort. The campaign involved hundreds of phone calls, along with 7,500 contacts by direct mail. They went out under the names of three different third-party sponsors.

We used three bios that had different slants on our client's experience. The results brought three attractive offers: CEO of a division of a large firm, dean of a graduate business school, and executive VP for a growth firm.

Summing Up

If you're seeking a six-figure position, you can afford to make an investment in a direct-mail campaign. However, don't make the mistake of thinking it will be easy. You'll need superior creative materials, the right mailing list, and an approach that's right for you.

If you can get five to ten leads out of every 1,000 pieces you distribute, you'll be doing all right. What's more, they're likely to be very good leads who need help right now.

11

Are You Willing to Aggressively Make the Most of the Phone?

Do you have a fear about prospecting via the phone? Or are you a master of this medium?

The new reality: Executives who are "pros" at aggressively using the phone are the ones who consistently generate the most activity. Reaching major players by telemarketing is your easiest way to generate interviews.

*S*ome people are totally confident in their ability to use the phone. However, 90% of executive job seekers are reluctant to make a "cold call."

Effective use of the phone is easier than you think. In fact, if you're not experienced at telemarketing yourself, believe it or not, it's a mostly friendly and helpful world out there. You will find that most other executives and their secretaries are courteous and polite.

Still, there is a misconception that secretaries will keep you from speaking with their bosses; they do screen calls, but they can also make sure contact is made.

Throughout this discussion, we'll refer to the term telemarketing. The difference between simply making phone calls and "telemarketing" is very basic. When you telemarket you have specific goals and you use a standardized procedure for making a larger number of calls.

> *"The problem for certain executives is that they don't understand that they better get to a state of mind that it's O.K. to call people... and the more the better."*
> —*Frank Reigel, Senior VP, Lockheed*

Can you stick to some proven telemarketing guidelines?

❑ Get used to making one call after another. Stand up and you'll give a power assist to your voice.

❑ Do your phone work in batches; you need only one success each time to sustain your morale.

❑ Plan how you will be answering your phone. Prepare answers to the difficult questions you expect.

❑ Prepare a 30-second commercial of your best selling-points. Rehearse it, tape it, and critique it.

❑ As you know, one of the best times to reach other executives is before 9:00 a.m. or after 5:00 p.m.

❑ Smile while speaking and your voice will sound pleasant. Be friendly, enthusiastic, and positive.

❑ Project a natural, confident tone—as when talking with a friend. Lower your voice and speak slowly.

❑ Be prepared for rejection. This is a numbers game.

❑ The secretary doesn't know who you are. If you only want information, the boss has no reason to shy away from you.

❑ When speaking with the secretary, get her name and use it. Be confident, positive and polite.

❏ Don't reveal too much of your story. You want to press only for an interview. Never be interviewed on the phone.

What are the easiest approaches for opening conversations?

The "good news" approach: Everyone likes to have good things happen and to hear from others who are enthusiastic about their good fortune. You can be sure that your message will help to build a feeling of friendliness and warmth over the phone. This kind of approach can play an important role in winning extra interviews and in getting people to help you.

> *"Mr. Ellis, when I heard about your four quarters of record growth…"*

The "third-party" approach: If you mention the name of a third party who knows the person you're calling, it helps to establish rapport, but it's also helpful even when they don't know each other. The approach is simple.

> *"Bill Regan, a partner with Andersen, thought I should get in touch with you. He felt your growth not only suggests a good investment, but might indicate a good employment possibility. His insights prompted me to follow up personally. Do you have a moment?"*

The "specific reason" approach: Anyone who has experience in getting things done can consider using this.

> *"Mr. Franklin, I have a specific reason for calling you. I know the business you are in and something of the processes you use. During the past 15 months, I have been able to save a company like yours approximately $850,000. I would like to share the details with you. Does your calendar permit a meeting later this week?"*

The "perhaps you can help me" approach can be used in just about any situation. For example, *"Hi, Mr. Ellis, I'm Tom Cole. Perhaps you can help me. Since the position has already been filled, could you refer me to..."*

"There really aren't very many executives who are persistent with their calls. They tend to give up too easily. I read that we received 1.5 million resumes in one year. But, if people can make calls without being obnoxious, they'll get an interview... sooner or later."

—*Anonymous Executive, IBM*

What are the basic strategies for handling people who screen your call?

❏ Use the name of the person who is the "screener." Once they are identified, people's manners become more personal.

❏ Identify yourself with an organization.

❏ Remember, the more difficult and expert the screener is, the more potentially valuable that person may eventually be.

❏ If you don't get through on your first attempt, suggest a time when you will call the screener back.

❏ When you call back, use the screener's name. If the person is difficult to reach, try this: "Since he's hard to reach, would you do me a small favor? May I call back at _____ to see if he would be free to speak with me for a few minutes?"

❏ If you must leave a message, leave one of potential benefit to the person you are calling.

❏ Consider reversing your attempt to speak with the decision-maker by asking for an internal referral to another line manager in the area in which you might want to work.

❏ If the screener refers you to the HR department, get the name of the person to whom you will be speaking. Call back later or request a transfer.

❏ Ask two or three penetrating questions about the company's needs. When asked difficult questions, people who don't know the answer are more inclined to refer you to the right person.

❏ After a few days, you can also call back the screener and explain that while the HR staff was helpful, they were not really able to answer the questions you had in mind.

❏ You may encounter the question, "Are you looking for a job?" The answer might be: "Yes, I am; do you think you could help me? A friend suggested your firm to me."

❏ Or you may encounter, "We don't have any openings at the present time." The response: "I appreciate a person who is direct; however, I have such a strong interest in the firm, I really believe I could be a great asset. May I tell you why?"

How about openers for after you reach the right person?

"Considering what is happening to the technology of your business, I know I can be very useful to you because of my training and experience in _____."

"In your Annual Report, I read that the company's expanding in the _____ area. That's an area where I could help, and I wanted to schedule an appointment."

"My friend _____ suggested that I make a point of contacting you. You may recall from my letter that I have experience in _____ that might be of help to you."

"With my background in _____ and the recent news about _____, I thought I should try to get in touch with you. Could you suggest a convenient time? Do you have 20 minutes before you get started some morning next week?"

"Mr. _____, your company has a tremendous reputation for market-leading products. I'd like very much to visit with you to explain how I could contribute to that reputation through my work in _____. Do you have a half hour free this Tuesday?"

There's obviously much more to telemarketing than I can address here. If getting on the phone does not come naturally to you, I suggest that you do a quick review of the many books devoted to this subject.

Summing Up

Being able to use the phone effectively is an essential part of every executive job search. You'll need to aggressively use the phone for setting up interviews, networking, and following up on your direct mail. Make it a point to become a "pro" on the phone. Your confidence will soar, and you'll save an enormous amount of job-search time.

12

Just How Important
Are Your Personal Contacts?

*Are you so well connected that you can de-
pend on your contacts introducing you to your
next six-figure position?*

*The new reality: There's nothing like personal
contacts; however, if you make the mistake of
depending on them, you could be in for a long
search. As important as they are, you need to
be aggressively using every other channel for
developing the right leads.*

*I*t wasn't too long ago that if you asked most executives
about the easiest way to find a new position, they would
tell you that the answer was credentials and connections.

What's more, the emphasis was clearly on connections. However, in today's environment, when the majority of executive job seekers must consider either changing
careers or changing industries, the importance of your
connections and credentials just isn't the same. As stated
earlier, when you go to market yourself, you must build
your appeal beyond your credentials, and you'll need to
market yourself with more than the help of your personal
contacts.

Nevertheless, before getting to the focus of this chapter, it's important to make sure you distinguish between using your most important resource, your personal contacts, and networking among strangers, which we will discuss in the next chapter.

"The key to executive job hunting has been, and always will be, personal contacts. You only do the other things if you don't have the contacts."

—Mark Westphal, Executive VP,
Major Steel Company

Let's face it, there's no substitute for personal contacts who can be of help. The best way to use them is to never ask them directly for a situation in their organization. At the executive level, the best way to use these people as a source of referrals is to ask their permission to possibly use them as a reference.

Most executives never get the most out of contacts they may have worked a lifetime to develop. Let me give you an example.

Have you ever heard an executive say, *"I've asked all of my friends to be on the lookout?"* They honestly believe they've done everything they can to get help. If they thought about it, they would realize that they have probably approached these friends on a very general basis and asked a favor which is next to impossible.

They say, *"Let me know if you hear of anything, Joe."* Joe, of course, will keep his friend in mind, but probably only for a very short time. Five minutes later, Joe is back to his routine, and his friend is forgotten.

However, the fact remains that Joe was probably willing and might have been able to help. How do you avoid the same mistake? Here are some simple principles that work. The first important thing you should do is select those who are likely to be your most effective supporters.

If you are a vice president, these people are likely to be presidents of companies. If you're a senior controller, it may be a VP of finance.

Make your request sound important, but make sure your communication is a pleasant experience for others. People are far more likely to respond if you make it easy for them to assist you.

For example, you might ask a past associate if he knows of any top executives among some growth companies you have identified. Or you could ask a financial executive to review recent financial job openings with you and request permission to use his/her name in a cover letter.

On the other hand, you could ask a senior executive at a former customer to arrange letters of introduction to companies in his field. Then offer to draft a letter. Or, if you know someone in human resources, you could see if he would help by lending his name for contacting recruiters. Let them know the jobs that interest you, the firms that have appeal, and just what you want them to do.

Aren't each of your good contacts a source of potential referrals... and a good reference?

Consider the story of Phil. His boss kept telling him he was worth more, but the firm was losing money. When

Phil heard that the company was to be sold, he felt his $100,000 salary was $30,000 less than it should be.

We helped make him aware of the power of his contacts. Would his boss, a good friend, be a good reference? And did the boss feel bad about paying him less than he was worth? Absolutely!

Could Phil ask him to be a reference, and would he raise him to a level of $130,000 in return for his staying for the last two months? Yes, and that is what Phil asked for and got!

Now, the boss had a friend who was a partner in an accounting firm. Phil asked his boss if he would approach his friend as a reference. Together, they visited over lunch. Guess what? He was happy to act as a second reference. In the same way, Phil developed a third reference, his own brother-in-law.

When he launched a campaign, he had a good interview with the president of a privately-owned paper company. A conservative man, he asked for three people who could speak about him. Phil immediately recontacted everyone so they were ready. After his boss had given him a glowing reference, the president mentioned that he was still uncertain.

When the second person (the boss's friend) was called he told the president that in the right situation Phil could help save a million dollars in taxes and control costs. He repositioned Phil in the eyes of this president, from a senior controller to a broader-based executive.

Next, Phil's third supporter endorsed what the others said and added a few points. Within days, he got a call from the president, and guess what? His message was,

"Phil, what will it take to get you?" Phil ended up with a position as VP finance at $130,000.

Can you make the maximum of your employer references?

Most of the time, important references will be the people you reported to in the past, the person you currently report to or their superiors, and, on rare occasions, the people who worked for you. Choose the highest level reference, as long as you get an enthusiastic endorsement, and avoid people who don't communicate well.

"What your references may say is very important, but the enthusiasm and conviction they project when they say it is even more important!"

—Charles Daniels,
Management Psychologist

The people you select should be personal contacts who know your background, are familiar with your achievements, and who have no hesitation in making strong statements about you. Even though you may never have worked for them, respected people in a scientific discipline, directors of trade associations, or magazine editors all might be of help.

By the way, the ideal number of references to provide will depend strictly on your situation. In most cases, three references will suffice. At other times, the psychology you use may affect your decision. One person gave eight references to an executive and suggested that he select two or three to contact personally.

Be sure to prepare your references with care. Let them know that you have high regard for them and for their opinions; this will reinforce the positive chemistry between the two of you and will make them want to do their best for you.

Don't forget that even good personal contacts will know only part of your background. Make sure that they learn the full story.

In the vast majority of situations, you will provide the names of your references rather than presenting letters of recommendation. In the nonprofit, academic, and government areas, however, it is traditional to collect written recommendations. These endorsements are frequently required in politically sensitive situations.

Another point is that some of your contacts are likely to be your best sources of referrals to employers. Leave them some resumes, and be sure to reassure them that you will not abuse the use of their names.

"We never hire someone at the senior level without checking their references. We let them know early on, and it's taken for granted, that sooner or later we'll ask to see a copy of their W-2 or income tax."
— *Ralph Gradishar, Division CFO, International Cosmetics Firm*

After calling your contacts, send a brief note that shows your appreciation and summarize a few positive things they can say about you. You can even prepare a list of questions that employers might ask and suggest some answers for them.

By the way, be sure to let your contacts know as soon as you have used their name, and ask them to let you know when they have been contacted. This is important because employers will sometimes ask them for someone else who is familiar with your performance.

When checking, people may look to discuss your management style, ethics, work habits, people skills, liabilities, etc., in addition to confirming dates and incomes.

Assume that employers will want to check with your past superiors. Track these people down for at least the last three jobs or ten years. Don't be reluctant, even if you have not bothered to keep in touch. People like to learn what is happening to others.

In the case of executives who have moved into top management, references from any but the last one or two positions are rarely needed. Let the employer know that you need to keep your activity confidential. This lets them know you have a worthwhile position to protect.

If you have worked in only one job or for one company for quite a long time, then contact former employees or bosses who have left your company and ask them to be references. If appropriate, consider using customers, suppliers, or trade group contacts.

Job seekers often struggle with concerns about bad or questionable endorsements. This is also true at the executive level. It's long been said that bad references won't hurt as much as the good ones that turn out to be poor. If someone is apt to give you a less-than-glowing recommendation, you need to bring it out in the interview and then supply enough people who will make good comments to offset it.

For example, if the interviewer asks to speak with someone who will be questionable, defuse the situation by explaining that you had differences of opinion on some managerial styles. Remain totally objective and unemotional, and never imply negatives about that person.

Also, you might have a friend do a mock reference check to find out what is being said. If the person is neutral, don't hesitate to ask the person to furnish more positive information. If necessary, explain that their input is keeping you from winning a position and enabling you to support yourself and your family. As a last resort, you may have to imply that you will seek a legal remedy.

Summing Up

There's nothing like personal contacts; however, before you approach them, make sure that your goals are clear and your materials are just right. Never ask them for a job, but do ask them to be a possible reference, and, of course, for referrals, and make it as easy as possible for them to help. Most of all, don't make the mistake of sitting back and waiting for this one lead source to work.

— 13 —

Is There an Easier Way to Do Executive Networking?

Besides using your existing contacts, are you willing to work at networking strangers? While there are a lot of other things you can do, it's still an effective method for searching out local executive positions.

The new reality: Many people have been networked to death; however, the amazing thing is that it still works very well. You need finesse, you need to be very clear about your objectives, and you need to use your time extremely well.

*N*etworking continues to be the most recommended way to get a new executive job. It's essential because it can dramatically increase your contacts and your chances for finding out about unadvertised jobs.

Networking involves establishing and using contacts to assist in your job search. By networking effectively, your phone presence, personality, and follow-through can substitute for a lack of the right experience.

There is a big difference between focused networking, which is clearly targeted by industry or involves influentials, and universal networking, which may be purely social or for advice purposes. The latter can take a long time.

Networking works because every organization experiences turnover—and a great deal more of it than they like to admit. That's why jobs are available with far more organizations over the course of a year than most people realize.

> *"Are you responsive to others who network you? Very much so. Who knows when I may be in the same position."*
> —*Fortune 500, VP Public Relations*

Focused networking has to do with quickly finding people who can refer you to others in the industry who might need someone like you. Networking within an industry where you have experience or interests and networking efforts directed to influential people are core parts of the system for a six-figure search. While this section reviews a broad base of potential networking actions, those are the two that will most likely merit some action on your part.

Now, even if you don't plan to change jobs again in the foreseeable future, start collecting business cards and keep your rolodex up to date. It works!

Pyramiding refers to capitalizing on the name of one individual to gain an interview with another. For example, if you were meeting with one firm, and you felt that the interview would not be productive, you could lead into a discussion about another firm.

You would then ask your interviewer whether or not he felt that it would be a firm for you to explore. He's likely to routinely say, *"Of course, you ought to contact them."*

Next you would write the president of the new firm something like the following:

> *"In my recent meeting with Mr. X, he suggested that it might be of value if I arranged to speak with you."*

Networking through influential people has been the key for many executives. Here is an example. A successful young executive from Boston wanted to relocate to Seattle. Unfortunately, she had no connections there. She launched a direct mail and follow-up telephone campaign, and within ten days she was able to generate six interviews through leads provided by board members of three banks.

Governors, congressional representatives, state senators, and other politicians can be excellent sources for referrals. The same is true for prominent doctors and lawyers who speak with many people during the course of each day.

Clergy, accountants, hospital trustees, members of the chamber of commerce or other civic groups, members of industrial development boards, investment bankers, insurance brokers and many others also fall into this category.

Another option is to expand your networking effectiveness through business activities. Here you simply have to increase your visibility. You can expand your business network by dining in restaurants patronized by those in your field, or attending seminars, parties and supplier meetings.

Anything you can do to gain visibility will result in easier initiation of new contacts. Taking an active role in community affairs, politics, and service clubs, along with speaking at seminars and trade associations, will serve as a means for accomplishing the same end.

Trade shows have long been an efficient medium for developing contacts. In one location, you usually have dozens of people assembled, and all of them are there because they want to talk to people.

"Absolutely the best way for executives to find jobs is to network with as many other executives as possible."
—*Bill Mattarick, VP HR, TRW, Inc.*

Still others have had success by networking through associations. Many professional organizations, alumni and trade associations act as intermediaries between job hunters and employers.

The executive directors of associations, chambers of commerce, and fraternal organizations or Jaycees usually have many "lines" into their communities. They know where growth is occurring.

Professional groups also fund and manage business magazines, journals, newsletters, membership lists, industry directories and trade show catalogs. The editors at these journals can be influential contacts.

Once you've made contact, the key to successful networking lies in asking the right questions. When probing for information from someone you don't know well, keep the questions broad, and related to the industry.

Naturally, you want to know about trends in any business in which you might to work. Questions like the ones that follow are suitable to ask of people whom you have only just met. They can facilitate the kind of shop talk shared at a trade conference.

If you requested a meeting for information and try to turn it into a job interview, it will look like you got through the door on false pretenses.

Here are some sample questions you might consider asking for general information:

What are some important long-term trends affecting your industry? With those trends in mind, what skills and expertise are companies apt to be looking for in new executives? What are some good sources of additional information—either articles and reports, or people to talk to? Who are the active recruiters in the industry? What are the fastest growing areas of the business?

When your network contact is interested enough to concentrate on your career needs, obviously a different set of questions is appropriate.

Can you follow these basic executive networking tips?

There are many common errors that people make while networking. Here are some points to remember.

❑ Getting through to people isn't the victory; that comes only after you've completed a successful interview.

❑ Be prepared. Decide what strengths to get across.

❑ Most people know when they're "being networked" and it still works, but you should never try to fool them.

❑ Talk with people wherever you go. Let people know that you are thinking about a new opportunity.

❑ Networking is part of the "job" of looking for a job. List the people you want to see, and find a way to get through.

❑ Remember to keep your interviews brief. Ask for ten-minute appointments. Send a thank-you note after your interview.

❑ Leave every meeting with several new names and be sure to make note of the names of secretaries.

❑ Exchange business cards with everyone you meet.

Summing Up

Networking strangers is a great deal more challenging than using your personal contacts. However, if you want a new position that allows you to stay in your current geographical area, networking is a must. In fact, whenever you are not involved with another campaign activity, you should work on actively expanding your local network.

— 14 —

Can You Create a Job and Be the Solution to a Problem?

Are you the type who is willing to wait for something to come your way? Or do you have enough initiative to create your own destiny?

The new reality: Knowing how to get a job created needs to be one of your capabilities. Let's face it, all of us have a propensity for hiring talent that comes to our attention.

You can get offers, even if no job openings are said to exist. You simply need to present yourself as a solution to a problem. The "create a job" approach is for executives who want a job tailored to their best abilities, or who may have difficulty winning offers through other means.

A few examples might include an executive who can develop new products for a company, a sales executive with contacts in particular markets or a general manager who can start up a division in a specific industry.

The "create a job" approach should also be considered by anyone who may have difficulty winning offers through other means. This includes those who have a narrow market for their talents; people who wish to change industries; or those who have been unemployed for a while or who want to stay in a specific geographic or industry area. In these situations, to win the job you want, you may have to create it by making an employer aware of your ability to make contributions.

Keep in mind this simple thought: Employers hire people whenever they are persuaded that the benefit of having them on board outweighs the dollar cost.

"I created most of my positions. When I moved to my senior VP position, I had gone to an annual meeting and met with a friend about the future of the company. The next thing I knew they found a role for me. Now I run the firm."

—*Anonymity requested*

The following pages will give you some guiding principles as you consider this approach. You must focus on small to medium-sized firms, go directly to people with the authority to create jobs, have a clear benefit proposition; take strong initiatives in your first meetings, and stir the employer's imagination.

Which companies are your highest-probability targets?

The first principle to understand is that to have your best chance at creating a job, your highest-probability targets are likely to be small to medium-sized companies. This includes firms that are growing rapidly, bringing out new products, forming new divisions, acquiring other companies or reorganizing.

These are the firms that need good people, often from other industries. They are free to move quickly. Large corporations are the least likely to respond to this approach. Budgets are usually allocated far in advance, and hiring practices tend to be relatively slow and methodical.

Of course, there are exceptions. All you need to do is assess your talents and contact the firms most likely to need you, regardless of their size or stability. And if you know a market well or have talents in a particular function, just consider the industries where they would apply.

Can you reach the individuals who really count?

The second principle involves your reaching the appropriate high-level people. For example, you must be able to communicate directly with the person you would most likely work for, or that person's boss. In small and medium-sized companies, it would be someone at the senior vice-presidential level or above. More often than not, the president would be involved.

Entrepreneurs, of course, can create jobs. So can affluent individuals who often have large staffs and interests in many organizations. In a larger company, be sure to choose the person who has ultimate responsibility for the area in which you can contribute.

When selecting the person to contact, aim on the high side. If you're not sure who to contact, start with the president. When you make contact at this level, you must be ready to communicate a benefit proposition.

Can you prepare a brief description of the benefits you can bring?

The third principle is to make sure that you get across your benefit proposition. It must be an accurate, concise, and easily understood description of what you can do.

> *"Some years ago, I hired a football coach from a little-known California university. The only reason I saw him was that he wrote such a good letter outlining what he thought he could do for us."*
>
> *—Owner, NFL football team*

Your message has to hold the promise of tangible value on a scale large enough to warrant an investment in you. In that initial communication, you will also need to establish your credentials. Mention specific results you achieved in the past. They are the best indicators of what you can do in the future.

If you're a VP finance, you will obviously want to talk about how you can save money by cutting expenses. But if you want someone to get interested enough to create a job for you, you'll stand a much better chance if you cite tangible results.

For example, your cost-cutting efforts led directly to a 5% increase in profits for your present employer; or your studies showed the firm was losing a million dollars a year on three product lines they could easily drop.

When you hold out the promise for potential benefits of that size, it is obvious to the reader that you might well be worth the investment.

Likewise, if you've developed many successful products, that is all well and good. However, if you expect someone to create a job, you'll stand a much better chance if you can state that you spearheaded development of three products now representing 20% of sales or that one now commands a 40% market share.

Achievements don't have to be large, but they do have to be significant. For instance, if you are an administrative executive, you might state that you managed a smooth introduction of new systems that lifted productivity 40%.

One key point to remember is that if you have an exciting idea to communicate, it may help if you can show how someone else has already used that idea successfully.

Dealing with opportunities is a key job for many executives. Most don't have enough time in the day and are predisposed to positive news from people who can help them. They will want to believe your message, so all you need do is make sure you provide positive reinforcement.

By the way, you can get your message across by phone or with a letter. Either way, make sure your "benefit position" is clear, easy to measure, and significant; and be prepared to quickly establish your credentials.

Can you prepare yourself to take strong initiatives in your first interview?

The fourth principle is to take strong initiatives in your first interview. Remember, your initial communication held out the promise of a major benefit. What are your ideas? What makes you confident they'll work? Do you understand the company's problems and opportunities?

Address these areas, but always remember to convey humility. Acknowledge that the interviewer has a better grasp of the problems facing the company than you could possibly have; this will help build positive rapport. There are any number of simple phrases you might use. For example, you might say:

"I hope you didn't find my letter too presumptuous. No doubt you've already given a lot of consideration to these areas."

Or... *"I took a calculated risk in telling you I could cut manufacturing costs. I recognize that every company is unique, and what works well in one may not work so easily in another."*

Or... *"I'm sure you've talked to many people who thought they knew your business better than you do. I don't mean to come across that way. I have a number of ideas, but let me first pay you the courtesy of listening to your opinion on these areas."*

Comments like these set the stage for a cordial exchange of ideas. They can allow you to do the three things you need to accomplish in your first meeting: learn what the employer really wants; build rapport; and focus the employer's attention on the areas where you can help.

Your first goal is to find out how the employer views the problem. What does he see as the key challenges? What is the "hot button"? Where are the priorities as the employer sees them? What attempts have been made in the past? And how much progress has already been made?

By asking a few questions and listening carefully, you will find out what the employer really wants. You will also be building rapport. Make sure you maintain a balanced conversation. Ask questions and make positive comments in response to the interviewer's remarks.

Most important, try to get the employer to share his innermost thoughts. Try to surface his vision for the organization. Only when he starts to think about this and the significant achievements he might realize, would he consider the possibility of creating a job.

If you are able to accomplish the above in the first interview, that is enough. State that you would like to give things some further thought and then clarify the benefits you might bring to the situation. Show your enthusiasm and get agreement that a second interview would be worthwhile. If you've done these things, you're well on your way to having a job created for you.

Remember, in your second interview you must reinforce your value by drawing an unusually clear picture of the benefits you can bring. Then you need to build enough enthusiasm to get an offer or be asked to speak with others.

Can you genuinely stir the employer's imagination?

The fifth overall principle involves your need to stir the employer's imagination. The employer should begin to anticipate specific benefits and be able to relate them directly to your talents. The entire focus of the conversation should be on the future, with the employer picturing a company already benefiting from your contributions.

> *"It was very rare. But any decision we made to create a job was as much emotional as it was intellectual."*
> —*Pete Sullivan, Former VP, AT & T*

A dry recitation of proposed improvements won't be enough. You will have to convey enthusiasm and create a sense of excitement. Of course, to do this you will have to refine your thinking, clearly identifying those areas the employer sees as most important. For each of them, be ready to discuss general approaches you would take to reinforce the notion that you will succeed. Your best way to do this is to tell stories about your past achievements.

If you build sufficient enthusiasm, the employer may conclude the meeting with a statement that he'd like to create a job for you. Or, he may ask you to meet with others in the company. If that happens, take the opportunity to build additional enthusiasm with every member of the team.

Keep in mind that if you're not getting interest, you might try the "report option." Here you need to make an offer to study the situation in more detail, perhaps to observe the company's operations or talk to knowledge-able outsiders, then to come back with a written report. The purpose? To make the entire subject more significant in the employer's mind.

"It is the same principle used by manage-ment consultants, advertising agencies, top sales producers, and others when they want to stimulate a company to action. The very act of a study, and the presenta-tion of a report following it, builds an aura of importance. Your report doesn't need to be lengthy, and it doesn't have to require a great deal of work."

—Bob Burnett, Sr. VP Outplacement, Princeton/Masters Atlanta

The report should, however, discuss the areas where you would hope to make significant contributions. For each area, you would want to point out how you would proceed, demonstrating carefully the near-term benefits for the company. If you get interesting input from outsiders or cite examples that support your points, it will make your presentation more compelling.

If you try the report option, be sure to stage it properly. Let the employer think it's important and ask for adequate time to present your findings. Your report, of course, would include a recommendation that a job be created. If the report is well received, you will have succeeded in creating a job.

Summing Up

Top management executives in most companies are well aware of the expenses involved in recruiting. When someone exceptional comes to their attention, many can and will act rapidly to create a job situation. This can involve the development of a new position or the shifting of someone of lesser talent in order to make room.

Every day, with a little imagination, people are winning executive positions created under these circumstances.

Is Your Resume
Compelling and Distinctive?

What do you think your realistic chances are of getting a six-figure job with an assembly-line resume?

The new reality: You are likely to need several biographies and up to ten different types of letters. If they don't present the right image, and if they don't tell your story in a highly distinctive and compelling way, you could be searching for a long, long time.

I always used to marvel at how bad some executives' resumes were, yet how well they did in the job market. Then one day I discovered that your need for a superior resume operated in reverse order to the following criteria.

First are those who have achieved what I call celebrity status. These are basically the executives whose reputations precede them.

Second are those who are well-enough known, or who have such extensive relationships that they can land jobs directly through their contacts. After all, when someone really knows you, they may not need a resume, or if they do, any summary you can put out will meet their needs.

Third are those who have an industry hook or high-demand specialty. Needless to say, if you're an expert on my business and I can use help, then let's talk.

Fourth are the top producers in any field, the people who can simply call and say, *"This is what I've done for others...I'm a pro...I can do the same or better for you."*

Now if you fit into one of the above categories, you can skip this discussion. If you are in the other 97%—then the information that follows is very important for you.

> *"I can't remember the last time US West hired an executive from an unsolicited resume. Sending one in is only slightly better than nothing."*
>
> *—Steve Wilson, Director HR, US West*
>
> *"Contrary to what you might assume, when I was at Xerox, we really did review every executive resume."*
>
> *—Doug Eiglehart, Management Consultant*

The number of resumes circulated, relative to the number of attractive executive jobs available, is going up. Hundreds of people are apt to answer every good ad.

As many as 4,000 resumes arrive each month at offices of some of the major executive search firms. In short, the competition is intense, and will continue to increase throughout the rest of this century.

When you look for a job, you are reduced to how you look on paper. Nevertheless, 95% of all executive resumes are far less effective than they could be. They are average in appearance, disclose too many liabilities and are rarely interesting. Worst of all, a single resume is usually expected to work with all types of audiences, and it doesn't!

Is there a single resume
style that's best for executives?

After applying a marketing microscope to more than 200,000 resumes, we have a good handle on what works for executives and what doesn't.

The answer: narrative resumes that are written in a style that is similar to a letter and that are almost always two pages. The length depends on the situation and how narrow or broad a person's market really is.

The first reason I prefer a narrative is because it seems like less of a sales pitch than resumes, which are full of dashes, bullets and too much bold type.

I know how much our clients want good jobs, but one of the keys is to never appear too available or a candidate for just anything. Who wants to hire someone who isn't wanted by others?

The resumes that work best are ones that make you sound articulate, that never simply scream a bunch of facts, and that tell a persuasive story.

The second reason I like a narrative is that it appears more personal, more dignified, and more professional. Needless to say, the closer it comes to a letter, the more personal and readable your resume will seem.

The third reason for a narrative approach is that it enables you to more easily avoid disclosing any liabilities you may have *(things that might rule you out and you'll never know why!)*

The fourth reason I prefer a narrative is that it is what I call a "solution resume." Using this style, you can craft the best story in support of any objective you have. What's more, if you decide on an alternate objective, such as a general manager instead of a VP sales, then it is relatively easy to shift it into a second compelling document.

The same holds true for preparing all the types of letters you might need in a job search. Once you have written your narrative resume, you can adapt the same words and phrases for your letters.

The fifth and last reason a narrative is the vitamin C for executive job hunters is that it simply works best in the four situations that you are likely to encounter.

One is when your resume is used as a leave-behind—after you've finished an interview, and when it is likely to be circulated to other executives along with the impressions of the first party.

A second is when it is requested after you meet an employer—at the beginning of or during an interview.

A third is when it is provided for personal contacts to distribute. And a fourth is when it is sent out cold to employers or recruiters—when it has to really perform.

If you give a moment to thinking about these situations, and you look at all the other styles you might use, you'll quickly see why a narrative is really the best solution—and truly the resume for all seasons.

Are there a set number of biographies you may require?

If you really want to make the most of your marketability, you will require a number of resumes. Here are the resumes most executives need in support of each objective in today's competitive marketplace.

First, you should have a very strong two-page narrative resume—one that can be used for your very best prospects in traditional industries and organizations. It could even go to three pages.

Second, if you want also to be a candidate for jobs in such fields as ad agencies, design firms, publishers, broadcasting, film studios, television, etc., then you'll need a narrative resume with more of a creative flair. After all, creative ability is more highly valued in those firms.

> *"I'd say you can't go wild with executive resumes, or you will leave the impression that you're overselling. The best compromise is to be creative yet professional; low-key but with a different look. Handwritten notes on the first page always get read!"*
>
> *—Gail Mendelson,*
> *Executive Recruiter*

Third, if you expect any results from executive recruiters, you will have to prepare a biography in a historical format. Recruiters are inundated by resumes, and their only interest is to quickly see if you are a good match for an assignment that they are currently seeking to fill.

Unfortunately, if you have a second career option you seriously wish to explore, you'll need another complete set of resumes that are geared to qualifying you for that career goal.

What's the best resume format for an executive?

Resume formats are simply different ways for arranging the presentation of your background. There are four standard formats. They include the historical format, the situation format, the achievement format and the functional format, which can emphasize skills or functions.

Your choice will depend on which assets or skills you wish to emphasize and which liabilities you need to downplay. Before you get started, make sure you are familiar with each one.

Once you've reviewed and decided on a format, you can lay out the framework for your resume, and then put the headings and subheadings in place.

Regardless of the format you've selected, your resume should normally start with your objective and a summary of your main selling points. Let's look at the four most popular formats.

"I don't bother reading anything from executives that is not a historical resume. The vague resume approach favored by certain outplacement companies doesn't do their clients any good with recruiters."

—Greg Peay, Executive Recruiter/President, Careers Ltd.

The historical format outlines your career in chronological order, starting with your most recent employer. It works best for executives whose careers include a succession of increasingly responsible positions. Clearly it is my preference for the simple reason that it is far easier to read than information presented in other formats. If you want action from recruiters, this format is a must.

The achievement format is most commonly used by people whose main accomplishments may not be in their most recent position. Here you simply list your achievements in the most persuasive language possible. Try to use specific numbers, time-frames, and percentages in describing achievements.

The functional format communicates your career experience according to "business functions" (sales, accounting, etc.). It's great for generalists, career changers, people who were with one firm a long time, and those with too many jobs.

You can use this same functional style and choose to emphasize skills rather than functions; for example, your experience and achievements in directing turn-arounds, boardroom presentations, complex analytical assignments, organizing new companies, etc.

The situation format tells a story about four or five key situations. It gives fast-moving explanations of those situations and how you dealt with them. This format can be very effective for executives who may be strong generalists as well as those in the highest echelons of corporate America.

Any executive resume needs to balance two considerations. Employers and recruiters need to quickly grasp the position you might be qualified for, as well as your most impressive qualifications.

Regardless of which of the four resume formats you choose, be sure to put an objective at the top of your resume, and follow it with a short but compelling summary. This tells the reader that you are an executive with a clear purpose, and it enables an employer to quickly assess you in terms of positions that may be available.

In your summary, you may choose to emphasize positive information on any aspect of your story, although most people will want to describe only work experience, education, and their most important personal assets. Having an objective and a summary will help ensure that your main selling points will almost always be read.

By the way, too often executives understate their contributions or give all of the credit to someone else. So, when you prepare your materials, take credit for larger achievements when you have played a key role in the overall effort. Try to quantify your achievements and measure them against some standard, i.e. annual, national, percentages, dollar increase or savings, etc.

It's also important that you present yourself as more interesting than your competition. You may also want to comment on issues that have potential emotional appeal; for example, commitment, values, motivation, professionalism, reputation, work style, interpersonal skills, among others.

"If you want to be successful, you need to beat your own drum. But you need to do it in a way that has just the right finesse. To be competitive today, your materials have to tell an extremely good story."

—*John Sherrill, Former VP, Broadcasting Company*

Is professional copywriting assistance a good investment for executives?

Considering what's at stake with a six-figure career, it's probably one of the best investments you can make. Why? Well, the main reason has to do with the sheer volume of superior resumes and letters that need to be created. Besides the biographies you need, you may need to compose up to ten different letters.

As I mentioned in the direct mail chapter, the letters are used for such things as answering ads; sending to HR executives, CEOs, COOs, and EVPs; emerging opportunities, networking associates, networking influentials, third-party letters; following up interviews; requesting references, and for contacting recruiters.

The craft of professional copywriting has to do with how well your key selling points can be assembled and presented.

In short, the writing has to be sufficient to immediately motivate someone to give you a call. To accomplish this, your communications must never undersell your capabilities or position you in an overly-narrow manner that might fail to reach the person you are addressing.

When I speak of professional copywriting, I don't mean hiring someone who will write your resume for $200. Furthermore, your average career or outplacement counselor will not have the combination of analytical insight and writing skills, and will never be able to deliver what you owe to yourself and your career. Remember, you are marketing a million dollar product.

What's required to do the job at your level starts with someone taking the time to understand your career situation and all that you have to offer the marketplace. Obviously, they need to be clear on what your objectives are, and they need to have the business vocabulary to create the documents you need.

For any good professional, it will take the better part of a day to study your situation and do what I have just mentioned, and then to deliver a first-rate biography. In a second and third day's work, a professional could create all the other biographies and a draft of the full range of letters you might require.

The cost? Anyone first-rate will cost $120 or more per hour. However, the value of the excellent creative materials simply cannot be understated. Your materials need to be persuasive; they need to tell your story just right; and they should make you sound like one-of-a-kind.

By the way, after you get a
new job, might you change positions again?

Remember the old expression KYRTD. It's been around for some time and stands for "Keep Your Resume Up-to-Date." One of the best things you can do for yourself and your career is to always have an updated narrative available and on hand.

As you go through your career, you're likely to become aware of attractive opportunities, but rarely will you be able to capitalize on them at the moment. If you make an effort, but you lack a superior biography, you will be handicapped by material that just doesn't cut it.

The kinds of situations I'm referring to include the occasional call from a recruiter, the opening that's come up with a competitor that is a level or two above where you are, the absolutely ideal ad you happen to see, the friend who tells you about an upcoming opportunity. I could go on, but I'm sure you've got the idea.

Make no mistake about it. Develop an excellent narrative for yourself. Then work it until it tells just the right story. Keep it on disk and update it from time to time. It just might make the difference.

Summing Up

There's nothing more important than making sure you conduct your search with the finest possible materials; they are the fuel that makes everything go according to plan. In today's executive marketplace, your materials need to be commanding, distinctive, and highly persuasive.

— 16 —

What Is Your Most Important Interviewing Strategy?

Do you want to spend time having friendly conversations? Or do you want to be in the first stage of closing your deal?

The new reality: With more executives to choose from, employers are increasingly more selective. At the six-figure level, 90% of job-hunting success depends on marketing and interviewing...perhaps 10% on background and ability.

*G*etting the right interviews is only half the battle. I'd like to now discuss just how you can stack the odds in your favor... converting interviews into offers at a higher rate than average. As a general rule, most six-figure executives require twelve or more situations to look into to develop a single offer. If you want to do better, your starting point is to have an interviewing game plan.

I'm always amazed at how many executives treat interviews as just conversations, while others treat them simply as sessions during which they have to answer questions. These things may happen, but an interview that turns into an offer involves far more.

Last year there were far more than 100 million executive-level interviews. Think about it! What's more, no two were the same. So how do you prepare? My philosophy is that you do it the same way you would prepare for a sports contest; there are millions of them and none are the same.

In either an interview or a sports contest, you can't plan precisely how things will go, but you can have a game plan. That means knowing the points you want to touch on and the pace you want to maintain.

Isn't the key to interviewing all about building personal chemistry?

Interviewing, of course, is a selling situation. But it's not only what you say that is important. Interviewing involves the exchange of information and the building of personal chemistry. This leads me to your first step for building chemistry, and it involves researching the company in advance.

"Nothing is ultimately more important than personal chemistry. When we got down to a few candidates, competency would rarely be the issue."

—Linc Ward, former VP & GM,
Pacific Bell

Did you ever meet an executive for the first time who knew a lot about you? It takes you by surprise, doesn't it? It's a great way to make a positive first impression.

Many people have built successful businesses that way. One friend of mine, a consultant with a substantial six-figure income, attributes his entire success to the research he does ahead of time.

Four out of every five of his clients tell him that he wins their business because he knows a lot more about them than anyone else does. So, let's start by having you make it your business to know as much as you can about the company, the industry, and, if possible, about the person you'll be meeting.

When you arrange or confirm an appointment, be sure to use the opportunity to gather more information. Many people have been able to get job descriptions, organization charts, and brochures ahead of time simply by requesting them over the phone. That will help prepare you to be able to build better chemistry in your interview.

What is your feeling about the front office staff?

Building chemistry with the front-office staff makes a difference. Can you guess what percent of executives say their secretaries influence them? What do you think? One-third? Half? Well, about two-thirds of them do.

Here's how this might affect you. Not too long ago, I was interrupted by Anthea, who stated that Mr. Baxter had arrived for his 2:00 interview. I had forgotten about the appointment, and it was a busy day. I immediately asked, "What do you think of him, Anthea?" She didn't say a word. She just gave a thumbs-down signal.

That was the end for poor Baxter. No one ever taught him how important it is to make a positive impression with the front-office staff. I told Anthea to have him see one of my assistants and to tell him her opinion first.

So please be attentive to the secretary and others who work up front. Remember, you can do more than make friends. Have a conversation that gives you information that will help in the interview. If you have to wait, and the secretary is too busy to talk, give the impression that you can put the waiting time to good use.

You may find, as many people have, that when you go out of your way to be respectful to them, they will often go out of their way to help you.

Is your attitude something you would be impressed with?

Every employer is looking for quality executives who can get the job done. So obviously you need to be communicating information, at all times, that establishes that you meet both of these criteria.

"This may sound extremely basic. We're a 'shirt-sleeves' company, but our executive selection process is heavy on image and attitude. Surprisingly, a lot of executives miss the cut on these factors. "

—Parker Tynen,
VP Sales, Microchip Company

However, building chemistry is also about attitude and image. My psychologist friends tell me that the way we expect to be treated affects the way we are treated. So build positive expectations about every interview.

Of course, you have to realize that when we are on the hiring end, as employers, many of us reach a negative decision in the first five minutes of an interview. Why? Well, if you have the credentials, you've either established a good initial impression or you haven't. And what determines this personal chemistry?

People silently react to the image you project, your posture and body language, the things you say about any subject at all, and the way you answer questions. So consider the kind of image you project. After all, each of us is continually projecting some kind of image.

It isn't just physical image or dress either, although your appearance speaks before you say a word. It's also a matter of attitude, interest, enthusiasm, and whether you come across as a person who is honest, loyal, and in good health. It even has to do with your outlook on life.

I tell my clients to check their image before they ever get to the interview, but they shouldn't be too kind to themselves.

You might go to someone who is not really close to you and ask them what kind of an attitude they think you project. Ask for their honest opinion of your appearance, eye contact, and mannerisms. Listen to what they have to say, then check out the same things with someone on your side. Somewhere between the two, there will be an accurate picture, and if anything needs to be worked on, do it.

Do you compliment others on a regular basis?

Do you like receiving compliments? Do you think other executives do? You bet they do. So before the interview, read or talk to people about the company and uncover some good things to say. Somewhere in those first few minutes, find the opportunity to let the interviewer know that you heard good things.

This will show that you know something about the company, and it's also what we call a "third-party compliment," where you are passing on the good news that you heard from others. You can compliment their facilities, people, products, advertising, public relations or anything else. However, whatever you do, be specific.

Don't just say that people you know are impressed by the product. Talk about "why" they are impressed. Maybe it's that new product they added, or the designs they've adapted. Or maybe it's the reliability of their products.

All of us like to hear about how our products have pleased customers. By giving details, you show that you have given the subject some thought and that your compliment is not just empty flattery.

When you answer questions, do you tell stories that are really memorable?

The way you answer questions has more to do with building positive chemistry than with what you say. For example, suppose you get the old standby, the number one question in the world of interviewing: "Tell me about yourself." Some people say that 25% of all interviews include a form of that question.

You'll want to answer, but chances are you're not sure what they want to hear. You could start out by talking about the kind of person you are and some of your attributes, but that may not be what the interviewer is interested in. Faced with such a dilemma, a safe way out is to self-qualify your answer:

> *"Certainly, Charles, I'd be happy to tell you about myself, and I'm sure you are interested in my work experience. I'll focus on the past few years and how they relate to this position. I can start with my most recent experience and work backwards if you like."*

136

When you self-qualify like that, you give the interviewer plenty of opportunity to respond, and to direct the conversation toward some other area, if that's not what he or she is really interested in. That way, you can avoid talking for ten minutes about the wrong things.

You will also want to answer questions with good, action-oriented stories. If you fail to tell a story, do you think the interviewer will remember the conversation? Don't bet on it. People don't remember answers to questions or concepts. What people remember and what impresses most of them are stories—good stories—action-oriented stories.

"After-dinner speakers know it, coaches, motivators, and preachers know it. Stories are the best way to make a point. So why not avoid the simple 'yes' answer and have stories ready to make your best points."

Bob Schrier, President,
Managing Director, Princeton/Masters
Southern California Operations

When you answer questions, remember to gear your comments to potential contributions relative to sales, profits, cost reduction, efficiency, innovations, quality improvement, etc.

When there is a silence, have questions about the field for which you have answers. Create an opportunity to demonstrate knowledge. Being prepared builds confidence and allows you to be more spontaneous. Always maintain eye contact and establish your sincerity and integrity.

When you encounter difficult questions, one way to handle them is with what I refer to as the "U-turn" technique. For example, let's say an interviewer says:

"You look very impressive on paper, Chuck. If you're this good, you ought to be able to solve all of our problems. Tell me, why should we hire you?"

Now of course you know the person doesn't believe you're that good. However, if you begin to talk about why they should hire you, you run the real risk of going on at length about all the wrong things. With the "U-turn" technique, you don't give an answer. Instead, you turn the question around in a way that acknowledges the status of the interviewer and maybe even pays an indirect compliment. Your comment might go something like this:

"I have a lot of experience I believe this firm could use. But it would be presumptuous of me to tell you what you need before I've even shown the courtesy of listening to what you think the priorities are. If you'd be kind enough to share some of your thoughts on these priorities, perhaps I could give a more intelligent answer."

With a response like that, you are very likely to get a knowing smile, often followed by a careful explanation of the way things really are in that company.

Can you find out what the interviewer wants... and let them know you have what it takes?

How do you find out what they want? Well, sometimes the interviewer will get directly to the point and tell you exactly what they are looking for. That makes it easy. Put your listening ability to work.

When you run into other executives who are not good interviewers, be ready to ask job-related questions that will start this person talking about the areas in which you can help the company.

Don't expect to be able to think of these questions in the interview, and be sure to keep them geared toward areas where you can help the company. One of the easiest ways to impress people is to ask intelligent and penetrating questions about the firm and the position.

Find out what happened to the last person in the job. Ask the interviewer about his experiences and that of his superiors. If a situation stalls, raise questions by simply asking what? when? where? why? and how?

Find out to whom the position reports and how long they have been in the job. Pinpoint the authority that goes with the job, and find out what they expect you to accomplish in the first six months.

You could ask a simple question such as, *"What would be the biggest challenge I would face?"* If the interviewer has some reservations, ask a question that is likely to bring them out. Don't forget—you're better off knowing their concerns so that you can deal with them.

"When it comes to executives, companies make their decisions based on the 'fit'— technical, cultural, and personal."

—Jack Bourque,
Management Recruiters

Most importantly, find out how the interviewer sees the problem, what their expectations are and what progress has been made. When you do this, you're learning what the unwritten requirements of the job are.

Let's assume that you've asked the right kinds of questions and done enough listening. Now you know what they want. It's time to let them know you have what they want, and you need to build chemistry as you do it.

To create this rapport calls for advance preparation. Ideally, at this stage you should have your own two-minute interviewing commercial ready to go. Again, the purpose is to let them know you have what they want!

One of the best ways to supply important information is with the action-oriented stories referred to earlier. After you've told your story, make sure you ask for feedback. You might ask, for instance, *"Is that the kind of approach you think you might need here?"* A positive response from the interviewer will help fix the story in his or her memory.

You will find that your conversations will follow a pattern. First, ask a question. Second, engage in conversation so you can listen. Third, get across that you have the required strengths. Fourth, ask a feedback question.

Now it's time to determine if you want the job, and you need to keep building chemistry while you do it. So, before the conclusion of any interview, you need to get some specific feedback. One way to do this is to verbalize a positive summary of the meeting, pointing out your enthusiasm about the job.

After the summary, ask a question that will generate feedback:

> *"In your opinion, are my skills and strengths as closely matched to your needs as I think they are? How can we pursue our interests further?"*

If you can build personal chemistry, as well as let the interviewer know what you want, your success may come down to projecting the right image. You want to be looking good and feeling confident, so be sure to dress well and try to get in the best shape you can.

When you have a game plan for building chemistry, you will project confidence from knowing what and how to communicate and being ready to do it.

Summing Up

When you're seeking a new position at the six-figure level, you always need to impress people with the fact that you are a quality person. You also need to build their confidence in you and leave them with the feeling that you are exactly what they are looking for.

However, thousands of executive job campaigns have produced convincing evidence that six-figure jobs are ultimately won by those who establish the best personal chemistry. The old adage is true: "People hire people they like."

— 17 —

In Interviews, Is There a
Simple Way to Handle Objections?

*Do you want to play it by ear when you are
thrown some difficult objections? Or do you
want to be ready to handle problems with ease
and finesse?*

*The new reality: With today's competition,
you're going to have to overcome every objection to win the six-figure position you want. If
you fumble or stumble... there are too many
others the employer can turn to.*

*T*he second key to becoming great at high-level interviewing is to handle whatever objections may come up—
and to do it in a way that is comfortable for you. Many of
us are more conscious of our liabilities than our strengths.
When confronted with a liability, we may become defensive, argumentative, or worst of all, acquiescent.

Can you handle an objection and
convert a liability into a perceived asset?

As I've mentioned, when faced with objections, the ten-
dency is to become defensive. However, no one sells anything to people while they are arguing with them.

> *"How good are the interviewing skills of the typical executive? The answer to your question reminds me of the title of an old Clint Eastwood movie...The Good, The Bad and The Ugly. While there are some polished pros out there, on the average, I'd say, 'definitely not great.'*
> *—Jonathan Williams, VP Staffing,*
> *Publishing Company*

You need to have a valid answer when an objection is raised, but jumping to the answer may seem defensive. To avoid that trap you can use a simple process I call ARTS. It can help you convert a liability into a perceived asset. The letters stand for the following:

A—Acknowledge the objection;

R—Redirect the person's concern;

T—Test to be sure you've removed his / her concern;

S—Use a story to make your point;

Whenever someone raises an objection, the tension level rises. What you want to achieve in step one is to reduce the tension level. Here's an example of acknowledging an objection:

> *"I can understand your concern. It is certainly something we should discuss, and I would like to address it directly for you." Or... "You're very perceptive, and you've raised an interesting point. It deserves some frank discussion, and I'd like to address it for you."*

The phrases you might use are not so important. Instead, it's the feeling you impart. You haven't gotten flustered. You have acted in a friendly and reassuring way; it's clear that you feel secure about your abilities in the area under question. Going further, here is an example of redirecting the person's concern:

"What qualities are you looking for in an ideal candidate that prompted you to bring this up?"

Let's say the interviewer raised the objection that your experience was in a different industry. Now, you can't do too much about the fact that your experience was in a different industry, but you probably can show that you are someone who contributes quickly, so that is where you want to direct the conversation.

For example, *"When you raise that question, I understand that you want to be sure the person you put in this job is someone who will contribute quickly. Isn't that it?"* The interviewer will reaffirm that you are indeed correct. Also, in case you did misinterpret, it will give him the chance to tell you so.

As you can see, with just a little thought it is very easy to refocus the conversation toward the positive qualities that are really on the interviewer's mind.

"Most executives think interviewing is a natural skill. It is not. Many people aren't good and never get better."
—Jim Moberg, Executive, Pacific Telesis

Here is an example of asking a testing question:

"If I could show that I could contribute quickly, even when it comes to learning a great deal of new information, would that help?"

After you get a positive response, you have the option of going directly to your answer, or you can introduce one of your key strengths. You might say:

145

"If I could show you that I work well under pressure, might that ease your concern somewhat?"

The final thing to do is to use a supporting story as part of your answer, ending it with a feedback question that will keep the conversation positive. Remember, what really counts is the fact that you did not get flustered. Instead, you had a friendly exchange in which you built positive feelings.

If you've done it right, interviewers won't be all that concerned about whether your answer is exactly correct. Instead, they'll be thinking, *"This person handled that situation very well."* Learn how to use this process, and for every concern, you should have your answer ready.

Summing Up

The second key to interviewing success rests with your ability as an executive to handle whatever objections may come up, and to do it in a way that is comfortable for you. Get used to the simple process I've outlined, and you will be amazed at how effective you will be.

Are You at Ease with the Negotiation Process?

What type of player are you? Are you happy just to get an offer? Or are you likely to be overly aggressive? Or perhaps you are a consummate strategist?

The new reality: Every executive thinks he or she is an expert at negotiating. However, the most successful negotiators are the ones who are very prepared, low-key, and never argumentative or emotional. What's more, they stick to a straightforward process that's easy to apply.

*T*here have been many books written by people who claim to be experts in negotiations, but they emphasize situations where you negotiate with someone you will never deal with again. Their philosophy is that winning is everything.

However, in the job search situation, the use of intimidation and attack strategies has no value. Techniques for one-upmanship can cost you the job. Here you're setting the tone for your long-term relationship.

It's important that you never allow yourself to be seen as overly aggressive. In fact, the reason most people don't like the term "negotiation" is that they associate it with confrontation, being tough and role playing something that does not come naturally.

The truth is, the best negotiators are very prepared... but low-key. They avoid anything that might cause irritation. So remember, never project an image of being even slightly argumentative or emotional. Follow the best negotiators and make sure you appear sincere and reasonable—never cold or calculating.

"Our offers always have room if an executive we want is good at negotiation. But if they're only earning $75,000 and looking for $150,000, they shouldn't waste their time."

—Carol Ritenhour, Executive Recruiter, Major Food Company

As far as the process is concerned, I shouldn't have to say it, but many people ruin things right from the start. You see, rule number one is to never negotiate until the employer is completely sold on you. Some people, though, misunderstand and think of negotiation as one continuous selling situation.

While there is some truth in this, you can't negotiate unless there is some hope that you can get the employer to offer new terms, and there is no chance they would offer you new terms unless they were already sold on you.

When you are ready to negotiate, the easiest way to strengthen your position is to emphasize that the opportunities where you are have some very attractive future possibilities.

Now of course you will find it helpful to have clear ideas about what you want. Realizing that you will not achieve everything, keep your main objectives in mind, and do not risk an entire negotiation by coming on too strong about less-important points.

Support what you want with only one or two strong reasons. The moment you give a weak reason, the employer can use that as an excuse for not granting the item in question.

Can you ask for what you want... without hesitation?

Assuming that you are at $100,000 or more, you didn't reach that level by being soft about going for what you wanted. So this is not the time to go in reverse.

Incidentally, no one will ever withdraw an offer because you ask for something in addition. You should always sell "quality" rather than "low starting price." After all, the easier you are to get, the less you'll be valued when you come aboard.

If you are looking to change for a financial reason, don't appear greedy, but looking for a 20% to 25% increase is acceptable. This is not to say it is easy, but don't lower your goals without first testing your marketability.

The key point to remember is that compensation for six-figure jobs is usually more flexible within the range that people have in mind.

Of course, if an employer is willing to create a new position to bring you aboard, that's always your best opportunity for negotiating something most attractive.

As a rule, you should also focus on negotiating a percent increase. For example, subject to how much you are currently earning, it is usually better to speak in terms of "percentages" rather than "tens of thousands of dollars." It sounds like less.

"It's always surprised me how much opportunity people leave on the negotiating tables. While there has been a lot written about it, I really don't think most executives attempt to negotiate. Frankly, we're in a retail business, and we expect people to negotiate. Sometimes we will change, sometimes we won't."

—Tom Ellis, Senior VP,
Major National Retail Organization

Also remember that if anyone has reason to suspect your earnings claim, they have a number of avenues open to them. They may ask to see a copy of your last income tax statement or your W-2 form, or they may also rely on an outside agency for a check on any earnings claim.

Can you express some vulnerability, and question rather than demand?

Expressing a slight amount of vulnerability can be a very effective weapon in your negotiation process. It is done simply by letting the employer know that accepting the job on the terms offered would cause you some personal difficulties.

This plays to the employer's desire to make sure you are happy, so you can devote your full energies to the job.

For example, you can be flattered by the offer, but you can say that you may have to sacrifice your current lifestyle in order to afford to take the job; and of course this would disappoint your family:

"I love the job and really want to join with you, but we'd have difficulty making ends meet. Is there a chance you could go a little higher?"

Questioning, rather than demanding, should always be the rule. The best negotiators persuade others through questions. This gives them the information they need to put themselves in control of the situation. It also gives them time to think and never has them putting all their cards on the table.

For instance, good negotiators will not say, "I do not agree with you because..." Rather, they will say, "Charles, you do make a good point, but I wonder if there is room for another point of view..." or, "I accept that point of view, but it raises a question about..."

They would never say, "That would not be any good for me." Instead, they might say, "Charles, could you tell me how you think this would work for me?"

Then they will follow up with questions, so the employer can discover for himself that the proposal is not quite good enough. And that is your goal: to let the company discover for themselves the validity of your request.

They might never be persuaded if you tell them their point of view is wrong, but if your questions lead them to discover it, they will be much more disposed to changing the terms. So remember, question—do not demand.

When it comes to discussing money, just how important is timing?

Premature discussions about money or benefits can be a real deal breaker. Besides, the more enthusiastic an employer becomes about you, the more likely he'll be willing to pay more. So learn how to avoid premature discussion of money. Sometimes an interviewer will begin with a statement like this:

> *"Jim, before we get started, I need to know how much money you are looking for. I don't want to waste our time if it is totally out of the ball park."*

The principle to keep in mind here is that you do not have to answer the question! For example, you could say:

> *"Charles, frankly, I could talk more intelligently about my circumstances after I know a bit more about the job responsibilities and the growth that's possible in this position. Speaking of that, I noticed that you listed technical experience as one of the requirements for the job. Will this job have line manufacturing responsibilities?"*

> *Or, "Charles, I appreciate your being direct. I would not take your time if I did not have a fairly good idea of the range you would be willing to pay. If we can agree that my experience fits your needs, I doubt we will have a problem on compensation.*

> *"Frankly, my concern is the basic question of whether your needs call for someone with my background. Incidentally, I've heard that you're entering a number of added markets with your new product. Is that where this job fits in?"*

Now, it is important to have your thoughts ready and to use words you feel comfortable with. Before the interview, figure out how you would handle the situation in your own words. That way, your response will come quite naturally. Once again, the U-turn strategy referred to earlier can help you here. It is a way to pleasantly avoid being the first to mention a figure. Here's how it works:

> *"For my part, I am most interested in finding a good situation in terms of challenge, growth possibilities and the people I am working with. So far, it seems that this position has it all. The company's commitment, the people, and my role in the overall effort all have great appeal.*

> *"And while money is important, I'm not locked into a specific figure because these other considerations are important. Now that you have brought the subject up, though, what kind of range did you have in mind?"*

Using this approach, you remain gracious and friendly while avoiding a direct answer. You will often find that the employer replies by giving you a stated range. If an interviewer persists about how much you earned or want to earn, you have to exercise judgment. Here is one possible response:

> *"I would rather avoid discussing my compensation until later on. Job content and challenge are most important to me, and I would like to talk money after I know you want me for the job. Is that agreeable to you?"*

If all else fails, give a range which surrounds your best estimate of the upper end of what the job might pay. By the way, making a decision at the time an offer is made can put you in a corner.

If you are offered a job, but the salary is too low, let the employer know how pleased you are they made an offer. Take the opportunity to praise the company and explain that you need some time to consider it. You might try a statement like this:

> *"Charles, I am pleased you made me an offer. This is an outstanding company, and the position has a great deal of promise. I am sure you can appreciate that I would like some time to give it further consideration. It would not present any problem, would it, if I were to get back to you tomorrow?"*

When you call back, after opening with one or two positive statements, consider raising the possibility of redefining the job. Your conversation might go something like this:

> *"Charles, I appreciate the fact that you gave me the time to consider the job further. As I said earlier, the idea of joining your firm is exciting, and the position is very appealing in many respects. I want the job, but I have difficulty with the level of starting salary. With children about to enter college, I had done some planning based on an income that was $10,000 higher. As I thought about that, however, I realized that jobs are not cast in bronze and that a company can often redefine a position to fit the talents of the person they want. Would it be possible to take another look at the job specs?*
>
> *"For my part, I know that if you could make a modest additional investment, I would show you a handsome return through my performance. I sincerely want to work for you and hope that we can make some adjustment. Can we take a look at it?"*

Of course, there may be situations where you do not want to redefine the job, but you would still like to raise the salary. In that case, you use the same technique, but show some vulnerability, then suggest that a specific dollar figure be added to the base salary.

Normally, if that figure is within 10% to 15% of what you have been offered, the employer will not take offense and will grant you at least a part of it.

Once again, the reason for the positive statement is to reassure the employer that you think the offer is fair. Asking for more money is a negative, and needs to be balanced by positives. If your positive comments are too brief, the employer would only hear the negative, the request for more money. Here is an approach to consider:

> *"Charles, I cannot tell you how pleased I am to receive this offer. The challenge is obviously there, and I think my experience is perfect for the job. What I am most enthusiastic about is that I felt such a positive chemistry with everyone I met.*
>
> *"There is one problem, however. You see, one of the main reasons I wanted to make a change was for financial balance. Can you see your way clear to adding $10,000 to the base? It would ease my family situation considerably."*

Isn't your enthusiasm
one of your best negotiating techniques?

Many executives forget to see the importance that enthusiasm plays in the negotiating process. Clearly, you should use your enthusiasm as a major negotiating technique.

If you load a maximum amount of enthusiasm into your statements, it becomes nearly impossible for the employer to conclude that you should not be with them.

Enthusiasm can be particularly important when you have been underpaid. Ideally, an offer should be based on your value to the company, but in reality, most employers will base their offers on present earnings.

When you get back to them, however, follow the principle of introducing other criteria on which to base the offer. This can include the importance of the job to the company, what you would make with a raise where you are, your total compensation package, what you believe the market is for persons with your background, or any other offers you are considering.

"We hire a lot of top sales executives. I'm always willing to listen, but I don't respond very well to people who come on too strong. There's a smart way to negotiate, but the wrong way could cost you the job."
—Bill Flavell, Senior VP,
International Business Development,
RR Donnelly

In the example that follows, notice how there are no demands, only questions. By your inviting employers to explore the situation with you, they are free to reach their own conclusions about whether their offer is too low.

Using this approach, you come across as easygoing, sincere and slightly vulnerable, never as cold, calculating or aggressively demanding, or as someone who is putting them in a corner. Your comment might be:

"Charles, let me first tell you once again how pleased I am that you made me an offer. I am very positive about the prospect of joining you. I've had the chance now to give it some more thought, and I can only say that my enthusiasm has continued to increase. If we can forget about money for the moment, this is

the job I want. It's the kind of situation where a person could look forward to staying with an exciting company for the long term.

"There is one hurdle that I have to overcome. You see, I've been underpaid now for some time, and it has created a financial situation where I need to start earning at a rate which reflects my ability to contribute.

"If I stayed where I am, I'd be due for a raise, which would put me close to your offer. But it's because I know I am worth more than that, that I want to make a move.

"In talking with other firms, I've discovered that some of them realize this, and they have mentioned ranges that are 25% higher. Now, I don't want to work for those organizations—I want to work for you. But I do have some financial needs that just won't go away.

"Is there some way we can get around this problem? Perhaps the company could approve a higher offer if they understood just how well qualified I am and how much I want to join the company. Can we pursue this together?"

Summing Up

To be predictably successful at negotiations, you need to be well prepared. You also need to follow a process that is comfortable for you to implement. The process I'm recommending is about common sense and soft selling. It has worked for thousands of others, and it will work for you.

— 19 —

Do You Know
What to Negotiate?

Have you thought things through, and are you really clear about what is being offered and what you want?

The new reality: Highly-structured organizations are fairly set in terms of what's open for discussion. However, with most other employers, the items that are possibilities have become a longer laundry list than ever before.

Can you negotiate the most important thing... the nature of the job?

Negotiating the nature of the job and its responsibilities is the most important factor you can accomplish. This is because the range in which you will negotiate compensation is determined by the responsibilities that go with the job. So, obviously, if you can reshape the job into a larger one, the salary range will be higher.

To get started, begin with a positive comment about the job and the firm; suggest that they might benefit by adding responsibilities to the job. Then offer to share your thoughts on what might be added. For example:

"Charles, there is no doubt that this is a good job. However, based on what you have told me, I believe I could be even more helpful if a few related elements were added. There are three areas where my experience could make a big difference. I'd like to discuss them, so we could see whether they could be included in the job description."

You could then go on to talk about the areas where the firm could capitalize on your experience, showing with personal stories how you have made contributions before. If the interviewer agrees these are important, have them added to the job description. Believe it or not, reshaping the job can often be just that simple.

"The vast majority of six-figure executives do negotiate, and probably successfully. However, we don't give perks away the way we used to: company cars, etc. The most common area of negotiation at high executive levels is the sign-on bonus. Certain people can have a high rate of success here because it doesn't throw our compensation and benefit plans out of balance."

—Senior VP, HR,
Telecommunications Company

Can you see from the example how some of the basic principles were applied? There was no confrontation. The manner was positive, friendly, and matter-of-fact.

Are you aware of all of the things you might be able to negotiate?

Base salary and commissions. Make sure that you fully understand any commission structure, as well as when and on what basis it is paid out. Clarify the timing of your reviews. Do you want to defer any type of compensation? Is there a possibility for an initial signing bonus?

Bonus. The object for most people will be to negotiate a bonus related to their accomplishments. However, if you are a superstar, you might try for a signing bonus. Mid-level people can also get signing bonuses if relocation or partial loss of pension is involved.

Profit-sharing pension plans. Your next employer may have a program. Tax laws now mandate vesting rights at five to seven years maximum. If you are negotiating a share of profits, you need to understand the accounting methods of the company to ensure the integrity of any understanding.

Medical, life insurance, dental, and vision coverage.

Severance payments. For senior executives, a standard agreement will cover two years compensation. This should apply if you lose your job for any cause other than an illegal action. It should also be triggered if the company lessens your responsibilities or relocates you. Some payments have included private school tuition for dependents.

Stock options purchase plans. The company may allow you to purchase stock at market price and have them buy an equal amount under your name up to a percentage of your income (e.g. 6% of annual income).

Stock grants. You may be able to negotiate stock as a gift. However, you will most likely be obligated to pay taxes based upon the market value of shares you are given.

ISOs (incentive stock options). Some companies have arrangements that allow you to be granted the option to purchase a certain number of shares at market value on a given day. Generally, they won't allow you to exercise the option to buy them for a couple of years. The primary value of ISOs is that should you eventually buy them, no tax is due on the day you purchase the shares.

Restricted stock units. Some firms will offer you an opportunity to receive stock units. They may peg the value of these units, for example, as one share of stock for every five units. The key is when you can convert to cash or shares.

"Chief executives' salaries and bonuses advanced 11.4% last year, the fastest clip since 1988."

— *From a survey by William M. Mercer Inc. for The Wall Street Journal*

Phantom stock options and stock appreciation rights. Here you negotiate the right to receive the difference in market value between your shares at the time you are granted these rights and their value at the subsequent time when you can convert the rights to shares or cash.

Non-qualified stock options. This is when a firm gives you an option to purchase stock below market prices. Whenever you exercise your options, tax will be due on the difference between the price at which you exercise your right of purchase and the market value of the stock.

Relocation expenses and other perks. This can include company purchase of your home, moving expenses; mortgage rate differential and prepayment penalty; real estate brokerage, closing costs, cost of bridge loan; trips to look for a home; lodging fees between homes; tuition; installation of appliances, drapes and carpets, spouse outplacement assistance.

Other executive perks can include automobile lease, country club membership, child care, annual physical exam, luncheon club membership, athletic club membership, disability pay, legal assistance, consumer product discounts, executive dining room privileges, financial planning assistance, tuition reimbursement, CPA and tax assistance, availability of short-term loans, insurance benefits after termination, outplacement assistance, and deferred compensation. Keep in mind that many perks may be out of reach because a company's policy may exclude them all.

Is it possible for you to negotiate some things in the future?

If you don't have any success in your negotiations, then you should shift from the "present" and focus instead on "futures" e.g. a review after six months, a better title, an automatic increase after twelve months, etc. These are easier things for an employer to give.

With inflation always a threat, the area of salary negotiations has become more fluid. Guidelines have been set aside by employers in order to attract good candidates.

Still, many people allow themselves to be deceived by discussions focusing on before-tax annual dollars. What you must be concerned with are the opportunities for improving your standard of living.

Before accepting an offer, you should calculate just what an increase means in terms of "added funds on a weekly or monthly basis"; this generally puts things into a much more meaningful perspective.

It also helps to take the time to write the positives and negatives on paper. While it is convenient if the highest offer is also the most attractive opportunity, things rarely work out that way. Once negotiations are completed, always be sure to confirm your understanding with a short letter.

Is a contract agreement
a possible consideration?

In recent years firms have been more open to employment contracts. In the past, contracts have usually guaranteed employees' compensation for a certain length of time, as long as executives worked "to the best of their ability during normal business hours."

Under the terms of most contracts, employers are guaranteed very little, and the executive can usually break a contract quite easily. On the other hand, corporations are often forced into a settlement if they dismiss an executive under a contract, and the courts tend to favor the individual in these matters.

"We will give contracts, but very few of our executives know which people have them. I can't imagine any CEO letting a real talent get away over a request for a contract."

—*President, Major Food Company*

Today, a contract is just one more element in your total negotiation package. It may be just as negotiable as questions relating to salary, bonuses, and stock option participation. If you can possibly arrange a contract, keep the following points in mind.

Keep the contract simple and try to keep your lawyer behind the scenes—out of the communication process.

Try to make sure the following are incorporated into the contract: the length of the agreement, your specific assignment, your title, location, who you report to, your compensation and what happens if there is a merger or if you are fired.

Some contracts can also cover bonus arrangements, deferred compensation, insurance, release with compensation in case of merger, salary benefits to your family in case of death, special reimbursement for foreign service, and outplacement in the event of termination.

From a company standpoint, you should expect that they will want you to enter a nondisclosure or trade secrecy agreement. This is a legitimate request.

You should always bring up the subject of a contract. A request, as opposed to a demand, will never result in a revoked job offer. In most large companies, both signing bonuses and severance packages are spreading down the ladder. This is especially true when relocation is involved.

Obviously, there are certain firms with which you must be very firm about a contract. These would include companies in financial trouble, acquisition candidates or those which have just been merged or been acquired, family-controlled organizations and companies where one individual dominates the environment.

In recent years, organizations have been putting new emphasis on agreements that will prevent fired executives form suing. Many firms insist that contracts includes language that mandates arbitration. The reason is simple. Legal disputes can be very costly for all concerned as they often take several years to wind their way through the legal process. As you might imagine, many attorney's counseling executives dislike artbitration clauses since individuals do better with juries where the emotional and antibusiness factors can come into play.

In any case, don't ever make the mistake of treating contract terms lightly, and be sure to review all the fine print with a lawyer.

If you can't get a formal contract, try for a termination agreement. These are substitutes for employment contracts. They are usually in the form of a short letter in which an employer agrees to irrevocable severance.

Many people favor the idea of these agreements. While few companies will acknowledge the fact, in some industries these agreements have already become quite common for salary levels above $100,000.

In most cases, such agreements provide for a minimum severance compensation of six months' salary, relocation expenses, insurance for twelve months and professional outplacement. Any agreement that you accept should cover all nonlegal situations under which an employer may choose to terminate your services.

Summing Up

When it comes to the items you might negotiate, there's a broader range of possibilities than ever before. As long as you've clearly thought through both your current situation and the realistic alternatives, you should be as ready as you can be.

What Do You Do If
You Lose Your Executive Job?

Are you going to take a vacation, feel sorry for yourself, and lose all your confidence? Or will you be ready to go to work, gain a competitive advantage and turn a liability into an asset?

The new reality: Three out of four people lose a job at least once in their career. And the higher you go, the greater the risk. Virtually every executive who becomes unemployed becomes re-employed. However, some do it quickly and successfully while others give up on themselves, settling for less than what they deserve. Your ability to bounce back will be the true test of your basic strength.

What are the most important considerations if you lose an executive job? Today, unemployment is looked at from a far different perspective than in years past. For the most part, someone who becomes unemployed is viewed as a victim of economics beyond anyone's control.

Nevertheless, for those who lose their jobs, there can be a feeling of shock, disbelief, and even fear. It can mean the loss of many symbols of security that we often take for granted. When we have a job, we have a place to go, an opportunity to achieve, tasks to fill our work day, and people to work with, including close friends.

"No one is secure in today's job market. If you're earning above $100,000, there will come a time when your position is re-engineered or the company downsizes you out."

—*The top HR Executive at one of America's 20 largest companies*

"If you lose your job, the big thing you need to worry about is to not fall into a comfort zone. That trap will lead you into inertia, becoming stale, and soon outdated. Be very active but not frenetic."

—*Ronald Stein,*
Senior VP, Brokerage Firm

Even in those cases where people resign, their initial feelings of self-confidence can quickly give way to concern and doubt if they don't land a new job quickly. Obviously, loss of income can also cause great apprehension.

Other people may not admit it, and may be quick to claim they quit all their previous positions, but many executives who will interview you will have shared the same experience at some stage in their career.

Being fired, or asked to leave, doesn't mean failure in the eyes of everyone else, even though you may feel tremendously depressed. Don't let it give you a complex and, even more important, don't feel sorry for yourself.

At senior levels in business, there have been many terminated executives that have gone on to further success. For example, Bernard Marcus, founder and CEO of Home Depot, Jimmy Johnson of the Dallas Cowboys, and Rick Miller, formerly of Wang and now CFO at AT & T.

Being unemployed does mean that you'll be carrying a handicap, as the great majority of firms prefer candidates who are presently employed.

What are the key steps you should take right away?

There are several steps that you should take right away. Don't vacation and don't retreat socially. Start on your campaign immediately, exercise regularly, and be as active as you can. Your advantage will be your ability to devote all of your time to job hunting.

Get access to an office phone. It helps to have a base of operations at an office. You might be able to use the number of a friend who can have his secretary take messages for you, or list a phone number (separate from your home phone) under your own consulting service. At the very least, establish a work station in your home and let everyone know it is to be treated as your office.

Get yourself an executive friend who will be a source of encouragement and who can be a good sounding board. It can be a relative, friend, or associate whom you respect. Share your progress and maintain communication with that person throughout the campaign.

Get support from your employer. In addition to out-placement assistance, they might even provide office space, secretarial help, and the use of a phone. Get total agreement on the reason for your separation. If there were negatives involved, work out an explanation that puts you in the best possible light. Look for clarification that the termination was due to factors beyond anyone's control, such as a cutback, merger or reorganization.

By the way, don't make the mistake of implying threats. If you are in a position to harm your employer, they will know about it without your saying so, and they'll be taking it into account in dealing with you.

"If a close friend lost a good executive job, what advice would you give? I know this sounds facetious, but the first thing I would say is that you should have launched your search before you lost your job. If you couldn't see it coming, you're not in tune with your organization or your boss.

"Get a strong support structure. Remain flexible. Slave over your materials until they are just right. Re-evaluate your campaign on a regular basis. Recognize that like major league ball players, you're simply now a free agent."

—Senior VP, Major Health Care Firm

Invest in your campaign right away. Review the chapter on outplacement and see if your past employer will pay for the cost. If the answer is no, you haven't lost anything.

You should also complete a financial plan that assumes that you may be unemployed for quite a while. In the course of planning, make sure you eliminate all unnecessary entertainment and household luxuries. However, allow sufficient funds to enable you to dress well, to get any professional help you need and to actively pursue a first-class job campaign.

Don't be overanxious. Never beg for a position or try to explain your situation in print. Everyone likes to hire talent that is hard to find. Don't show up in advance of your scheduled interviews, and don't always be available at the first suggested time for further interviews.

Be as active as you can. Many executives who have not been active have found that as more time passed, the less capable they were—psychologically and emotionally—to go out and do what must be done to win the right new job.

The best psychological boost you can get will come from having a schedule of full activity: breakfast meetings, business lunches, interviews, letter writing, phone calls, follow-ups and negotiations. The way to do that is to get into action and give your job search top priority. This is no time to fix up the house!

As important as your assets and skills are, you also need to be aware of anything that might be viewed as a shortcoming in the eyes of potential employers. Sometimes liabilities are overlooked. On other occasions they are mistakenly thought to be so serious that job hunters conclude that no corrective action can be taken.

To be successful, you should develop your strategy for handling any potential liability before you ever write your resume or get involved in interviews. You know what your problem areas are. Give some careful thought about how you should minimize their impact in all of your communications... both written and verbal.

By the way, some of the common liabilities that can cause a negative perception include: you're unemployed; you'll need to change industries; you've stayed too long with one employer; you're too old; you've changed jobs too often; you may be too generalized or too specialized; your career has peaked; your achievements aren't measurable; you lack experience in blue-chip firms; your jobs have been too similar; and your work history has gaps. Keep in mind that there is virtually no career problem that has not already been successfully resolved by someone else.

Why not approach your success as being inevitable?

If you build your will to succeed, it will make the difference every time. Your positive attitude is what will drive you to do it sooner rather than later. It is the single most common thread among all winners. It will separate you from the tens of thousands who simply give up, settle for less, or remain in unattractive situations.

"It's very clear that the beliefs we hold have a lot to do with the kind of world we experience. If, for example, you believe the economy is bad and firms are not hiring, you will go through the news and pay attention to items about layoffs or declines in sales. On the other hand, if you believe that there are many areas of opportunity, then you will seek out new companies, new products and the like."

Stephanie Miller, Psychologist

Now, it won't be news to you that if you truly believe in yourself, you will have the best possible chance of achieving the most you are capable of. So it's a good time to remind yourself of all of the good things you have done, and what you can do in the future.

Look again at your negative thoughts. Then start to realize that you can change your beliefs about the way things are. It's very simple. Write down the positive side of every negative belief. You will be left with positive beliefs, which is where you want to be.

The best way to make things happen is simply to get into action. Too many people make excuses. If it's not a recession, then it's their industry. If not that, then their skills have been made obsolete by technology. If not that, there are too many people going after too few jobs. There is no end to the power of rationalizing. Of course, these people lose their will to succeed and become immobile.

If, on the other hand, you look at the lives of achievers in any field, you will see that in addition to positive expectations, another common thread is they are very active people. Taking action is in itself like taking an energy tonic. When people get into action, they no longer have time to worry about whether they will achieve their goal.

Don't let life go by without doing the things you really want. To get the right job, you need the right attitude to get going, as well as the determination to do your best. Then you need to project the right attitude with everyone you meet. In short, it's your attitude that makes the sale. It works!

Summing Up

If you lose your job there are some basic steps to take right away. How you handle matters can have a major impact on your financial situation, the length of time you spend between careers, and your chances for finding a job at the level you want.

Losing an executive position is so commonplace today that the guidelines are clear. Follow this chapter and you'll save yourself from a great deal of strain, confusion and worry.

— 21 —

Is Professional Help
the Right Option for You?

What's your career worth at this stage? How much of an investment are you willing to make to increase the odds for getting what you want?

The new reality: Some outplacement is more than worth it... and much of it isn't. But since every six-figure executives' time is worth $2,000, $3,000 or more every week, you can save considerable time and money with marketing help in several key areas.

*T*he term *outplacement* was first coined more than 25 years ago. While many people retain outplacement services privately, the term itself denotes the process whereby employers sponsor job search assistance for employees they terminate.

If by chance you are not familiar with this industry, you might be wondering why employers would pay to help people when they are downsizing. It begins with the difficulty of letting people go. Many employers provide this service because they want to ease the process.

Others provide it to reduce legal exposure and to show those who remain that the company treats people fairly. Still others provide outplacement to keep good public relations and, of course, to help people become reemployed with a minimum of stress and bad feelings.

Today, private and corporate outplacement is a billion dollar industry. Outplacement is gradually finding its way into the American corporate culture as a standard benefit. Unfortunately, the term itself can easily mislead people.

"My experience with outplacement firms is mixed. If the wrong organization is selected, it's just money down the tubes."
—*Steve Massina, Senior VP, Home Depot*

Outplacement services involve helping people help themselves to find a new job. No one does it for you or places you! Until recently, most services simply involved having a counselor teach you about job hunting and then act as a sounding board throughout your search.

However, the major need of six-figure professionals involves finding executive assistance that really helps market them into a new situation.

There are many good outplacement consultants, but their resources and the nature of their services can differ dramatically. Let's look at the range of assistance that is available to six-figure executives, including what may be worth it...or not!

Here's the "worth it" list; every six-figure executive should consider getting help in these key areas.

Having your situation analyzed.

Minimally, any reputable outplacement service should be able to go to work immediately and develop a platform from which you can launch a serious campaign effort.

The initial objective is to bring to the surface everything that you have to offer a potential employer, lay out the full range of your career and industry options, and help you settle on specific goals.

Once these goals are met, they would also give you a recommended plan of action... a blueprint, if you will. This would include a step-by-step listing of everything that needs to be done to generate the right interviews. By everything, I mean a detailed "what," "when,"and "where" plan.

Having your creative materials prepared.

Obviously, by now you know my feelings about this. Any six-figure executive is taking an unnecessary risk by writing all of his or her own materials.

If you choose this option, ask the firm you are considering to show you a full set of the creative materials they have written for another client, and then judge for yourself as to the caliber of their work.

It will take any good professional 15 to 20 hours to fully analyze your situation and then to turn out a full set of bio-narrative resumes and drafts of customized letters to fit all your needs.

Identifying the right contacts.

With today's range of databases that are available, any outplacement firm worth its weight will have no problem quickly compiling most of the information you require. On your own, this could take weeks of library time. Even then, quite frankly, you couldn't match what could be done for you in this regard.

If possible, you also want to get hold of reports on emerging opportunities. This research can be of great help if you want to find a position in a specific metropolitan area. Here various outplacement firms have their staffs review all of the business press on a daily basis. They search out any news event that might be a lead to unadvertised opportunity and enter it into their database.

These reports can bring you current on what's been happening in the local marketplace for the last several months. If you are relocating to an area where you don't have a network, this can be especially valuable.

Providing counsel throughout the campaign

The most important thing that outplacement firms do is to make available their professional counsel. Having a knowledgeable consultant in your corner can make an enormous difference. However, your requirement for lengthy or ongoing counsel, as opposed to another executive's, may vary considerably.

On a less critical level, certain executives may find themselves quite rusty in interviews. In just a single video session, a good consultant can help you correct bad habits and project a better image. Many feel this is helpful; others may not really need it.

One other area of service that certain outplacement firms offer is various forms of aptitude or psychological testing, therapy from psychologists, and the like. Only a small percentage of six-figure executives will benefit from this help.

Campaign implementation
and executive suite services

A full professional search on a national level can involve direct mail marketing to up to thousands of organizations. Having the mailing done for you can save an enormous amount of time; however, you don't need it if your career specialty is such that a small, highly targeted mail campaign is in order.

For certain people who are out of work, or about to be, having access to office space, phone and word processing services can also be a great advantage.

Here's the "not worth it" list... services
that can often be disappointing investments.

First on my list are the outplacement services that won't actually do the full writing and research for you. These firms "show you" how to do it, leaving you with all the work. They also frequently put all their emphasis on showing you how to network more effectively. Obviously, networking is largely a local activity, one where all the burden is on you.

Second on my list are firms who give six-figure executives advice, but who never put their assessment and marketing-plan recommendations into writing.

Third are those who will write your resumes and letters, but who turn out standard form material, or what

I refer to as job-hunting junk mail. The only writing worthwhile is from professionals who spend the time to study your situation and who can really prepare customized work to meet your needs.

Critics of corporate-sponsored outplacement point out that from an individual's standpoint, the trouble is that it's a service bought by someone other than the person being serviced. This is a valid concern. Unfortunately, many companies still pay more than necessary... and often for services that give the executive considerably less than what I am recommending.

If you are interested in professional assistance, consider two last points.

Make sure the professional firm you are considering gives you literature describing their service and be wary if they don't have any or say they don't use any. When you do look at their material, review it carefully. If they don't do an impressive job of marketing themselves, they'll never do any better for you!

Secondly, make sure they warranty your satisfaction with every phase of their service. If you are not satisfied, will they do the work over again until you are satisfied? If the campaign they design does not work, will they develop a new campaign? If necessary, will they also create all new resumes and letters and provide fresh research?

You should expect these warranties from any reputable firm you select, and they should give you confirmation of their warranty in writing. With the right marketing support, professional outplacement can save you a significant amount of time, especially if you are looking while you are currently employed.

**Everyone's career is their best investment—
can we be of assistance?**

Our customized outplacement marketing services were
developed to meet the needs of employers and their executives
who wish to save time and money in today's marketplace.

Most of our assignments have us take a role as senior
level Marketing Directors for our clients. The team that
we draw upon for these assignments includes more than
275 executive problem-solvers, marketing experts, professional
copywriters, and administrators.

In our world of overnight deliveries, faxes and advanced
telecommunications, we manage campaigns for
executives throughout the world, regardless of their geographic
proximity to our offices.

If you or your company would like help in outplacing
six- figure executives, please give us a call.

**For descriptive literature or more information
call Peter Bennett Mills at 1-800-772-4446**